WALKING THE CAMINO

WALKING
THE CAMINO

A JOURNEY FOR THE HEART AND SOUL

Julia Goodfellow-Smith

Walking the Camino: A Journey for the Heart and Soul
Published by Julia Goodfellow-Smith

First published in 2023
Copyright © Julia Goodfellow-Smith

ISBN – paperback: 978-0-86319-488-7
ISBN – e-book: 978-0-86319-489-4
ISBN – large print: 978-0-86319-492-4

Walking the Camino is dedicated to Hazel,
for introducing me to the Camino and the joys
of long-distance walking.

Table of Contents

Divine Intervention?

'Bye, Julia! See you in six weeks.'

We hugged. 'Have a great trip.'

On the way home, I mulled over what my friend Hazel had said. She was about to embark on the Camino de Santiago. I had never met a woman who had walked that far before, or who would consider doing so on her own.

Decades ago, I had spent a miserable week walking the Yorkshire Wolds Way with a friend. Rather than learning from my mistakes, I had simply sworn never to do anything like that again.

Why would anyone tackle a route like this? What was she hoping to gain from it? It wasn't just the distance, it was the number of people too. Over 100,000 pilgrims walk the Camino every year. Think of the crowds!

When Hazel returned, she was glowing.

Her experience on the Camino sowed a tiny seed in my mind. Over the years, the idea of walking long distances morphed from a dread into a dream and became a reality. First, three days from London to Sussex with my husband Mike. Then, nine days from Malvern to Liverpool with Hazel. Eventually, my confidence grew enough to walk the 630-mile South West Coast Path in its entirety one autumn.

During this period, my curiosity about the concept of pilgrimage grew. Would a pilgrimage be any different to other long-distance walks? When I heard that Alexander Chapman Campbell wrote *A Journey to Nidaros* while on a pilgrimage in Norway, I bought the album. The music is calming, haunting and beautiful. If he was inspired to create something this sublime on pilgrimage, perhaps it was worth considering.

Hazel planned to return to the Camino with her friend Frank. She invited me to join them. I demurred. All those people!

But the seed of pilgrimage was firmly lodged in my mind. And slowly but surely, as I got my walking legs, the seed grew and a green shoot started to unfurl its leaves.

Perhaps it was divine intervention. After all, they say that the Camino gives you what you need, not what you want. I was due to be hiking in Costa Rica when Hazel was planning to walk the Camino for the second time. At short notice, the Costa Rica trip was cancelled.

I was hiking fit and had been learning Spanish. This time, when Hazel invited me to join her, I readily agreed. It was a turn-key trip. I had already done all the preparation I needed except for booking the flights.

The deal was done. It was time to find out what all the fuss was about and experience pilgrimage first-hand. Hazel was setting off immediately. I started to count down the days until I could join her.

Section 1:

My Summer Camino

Discombobulation

As the plane touches down, the familiar butterflies are back in my ribcage. A new adventure is starting!

I remain curious about the Camino. Why does it attract so many people, whether Christian or not? Will it be any different to other long-distance walks?

When Hazel returned from her first Camino, she told me that most pilgrims carry a stone that represents a burden to leave behind at the Cruz de Ferro, the Iron Cross. My fingers run over the smooth surface of the pebble that I have brought for that purpose. It isn't yet clear to me what my burden is. The obvious one is grief for my mother, who died when she was just a few years older than I am now. But I suspect it might be something else that has yet to reveal itself. There are a couple of weeks to walk before we reach the cross, so hopefully, all will become clear in that time.

As usual, the lead-up to setting off has been hectic. I am in the middle of buying a house, have just submitted a finished manuscript to a publisher and have been attempting to unpick the trip to Costa Rica. Fractured thoughts flit around my brain like bats in an insect-laden sky. I am looking forward to this time away from the usual pressures and distractions of life to recreate some order from the chaos.

I notice that I am holding two completely contradictory emotions at once. As I step off the bus at the Guggenheim Museum in Bilbao, my heart fills with the glee of being in a different country, somewhere just a little bit different to home. That feeling is joined, rather than tempered by, trepidation as I limp forward, very aware of my aching right hip.

Two of my school friends have already had hips replaced, and I fear that I am on the same slippery slope. Perhaps it is foolish to attempt a 500km hike in these circumstances, but in the past, walking has eased the pain. Will it help this time, too?

'Julia, you've got this.'

It's only day zero, and the mantra I adopted while walking the South West Coast Path is already in play!

I hobble around outside the museum. An enormous spider looms over the riverside path, ready to pounce. The effect is exacerbated when fog starts to swirl around its spindly legs. In contrast, the metallic jewel-coloured blobs reflecting in the pond are joyful. A giant floral dog guards the entrance, as far from a fierce, snarling guard dog as it's possible to get. This place is designed to mess with your mind. The feeling of being inside a surrealist painting intensifies with the building itself, which is both angular and curvy, glistening in the sun.

On entering the museum, I have high expectations and the structure does not disappoint. The spaces feel surreal yet familiar, awe-inspiring yet comfortable. On the other hand, the art exhibitions leave me cold.

Except for one.

The steel sculptures catch my eye from a balcony and draw me towards them. I race downstairs to find the exhibition, my heart thumping in anticipation.

The first sculpture draws me in a spiral right into its heart. It sounds simple, but it isn't. The walls of the spiral sometimes lean out and sometimes in. In places, it feels like the walls are closing in, and I have to fight back panic. Just a few paces further on, there is room to breathe and enjoy the expansive space over my head. Once in, there is only one way out – back round the same confusing spiral, playing with my emotions.

What a crazy ride – where's the next one?! The cavernous exhibition hall contains spirals, ovals and ripples. Sometimes I walk slowly, brushing the rough steel with my fingertips. Sometimes I run. I find myself leaning first one way, then the next, as my mind and body try to adjust to the shifting reality of the surroundings. It is totally discombobulating and completely awesome!

Little do I realise that this is much what the experience of walking the Camino is going to be like.

An Inauspicious Start

'¿Discúlpame, este tren va a Briviesca?' Does this train go to Briviesca?

It looks like my Spanish lessons are going to come in handy. It is taking longer than expected to reach the next station, my final destination. In stilted Spanish, I converse with some other passengers and find that I have boarded a train that is heading in the opposite direction.

It's a long way to the next station, and the train I missed was the last one today. I take a deep breath and force a smile. It's time to revise my plans. There's a train to Burgos I can catch. It will have to do – it's as close as I can get today.

At the station, the ticket office is closed and the machine doesn't work. Time for a bit of positive self-talk. 'Julia, you've got this. You can always buy a ticket on the train. What's the worst that can happen?'

I step onto the train, find a seat and plonk myself down, relieved to be heading in approximately the right direction again.

The seats are big and comfortable; much better than those in the UK.

'I'm sorry, I don't have a ticket. The machine was broken.' I flash my brightest smile and very best Spanish at the conductor. Time for a charm offensive. He has to explain twice before I understand enough to realise that I am sitting in first class. No wonder the seats are so spacious!

He takes me to another carriage and sells me a ticket, while I explain that I am a pilgrim, about to embark on the Camino. He was already courteous, but at this, his courtesy tops the scale.

'A pilgrim! That's fantastic! I have a house on the coastal Camino.'

He scurries off to see to the rest of his ticket collection duties, while I start to relax. I cannot believe that I have just managed to hold a conversation with two sets of people in Spanish.

'You really have got this, Julia!'

The conductor reappears and shows me some photos of his house on the coastal route. He is talking fast now, so I don't catch everything he says, but I get the gist of it. The house is small and rustic, with a Camino waymarker on the wall. The area looks delightful – I mentally add the coastal route to my bucket list. As he departs, he delivers a heart-felt '¡Buen Camino!', the pilgrim greeting.

In the taxi on the way to meet up with Hazel, with the landscape whizzing past and the meter rising just as fast, a sense of dread starts to weigh me down. What am I doing? Hazel has told me that she is now walking with a Camino 'family' – Catarina and Brad have joined her and Frank.

How will I cope with being in company hour after hour, day after day? Will I like the other two? Will they like me? They have been walking together for ten days already. Will my arrival upset their group dynamics? It feels like the first day at a new school, where you don't know how anything works, and it's already mid-term.

I am learning that confidence is something that ebbs and flows, depending on many different factors. Right now, it is ebbing strongly, but I will just have to 'woman up' and get on with my new pilgrim life. I have made my bed, and now I need to lie on it.

I arrive just in time to receive the first stamp on my new pilgrim passport and grab a shower before meeting up with the others.

'It's so good to see you, Julia.' What a lovely greeting from Hazel, accompanied by a strong hug. 'Let me introduce you to the rest of my Camino family.'

I have met Frank once before, at a wedding. He was laid-back and twinkly that night. Nothing has changed, even though he's two weeks into the walk and his feet are in a bad way.

Catarina is Swedish and seems friendly, naturally accepting a hug in greeting. Brad looks baffled at the suggestion of a hug but opens his arms to accept one anyway.

It's almost lights-out time. 'What should I wear to sleep in?'

'It's far too hot to contemplate anything but underwear.'

It takes a few minutes to organise my bag ready for a quick exit in the morning. I undress and slip into my sheet sleeping bag as quickly as possible. It is a mixed dorm, after all.

'Don't worry about setting an alarm in the morning, Julia. Brad will wake us all up at 5.15 a.m.'

5.15 a.m.! Goodness – it's a good job that lights out is so early!

The main lights are switched off, but all night, it seems that someone is walking around with a headtorch on, despite plenty of ambient light, flashing it around the room and into my eyes. Multiple people are snoring. The door into the corridor is opened and closed numerous times. The pain in my hip is not helping, either. I scrunch my eyes shut and try to relax.

At 4.45 a.m., an alarm jolts me and the rest of the room from our slumbers. The guilty pilgrim turns on the light above her bed and proceeds to pack noisily. The whole dorm is woken. I turn away from the light and noise and fall back into a deep sleep.

'Why is everything shaking?' I wonder through a sleep-drenched haze until finally, I realise that it is not a dream. Brad has hold of my shoulder and is shaking me hard.

'Morning!' A very quiet whisper right in my ear. I turn to see him smiling. I interpret the smile as friendliness, but later find it is relief that I have finally woken up.

I dress as quickly and quietly as possible, not wanting to disturb everyone in the dorm again, scoop up my bedding and rucksack, and tiptoe from the room. Out of sight and earshot, we all pack our bags, a routine that I guess will become familiar: Stuff the blanket back into its sack, roll up the sheet sleeping bag, check the water bladder is full, drink half a litre so I'm not starting the day dehydrated, refill the water bottle, splash some water on my face, clean my teeth.

We're soon ready to leave. It's time for my pilgrimage to begin in earnest.

Meeting Lloyd

Spain is gripped by a heatwave and my Camino family has been walking in searing temperatures. They have been setting off early to avoid walking in the hottest part of the day. I step out of the front door expecting to be wrapped in warm air. It takes a few moments for me to realise. It's drizzling. My heart sinks. This is just like the weather I left behind in England!

Oh well, it probably won't last for long. I drop my rucksack, pull the rain cover over it and hoick it back onto my shoulders. Despite the damp, a smile tickles my lips. After training hard, my pack feels light and comfortable. Carrying a pack as light as this is going to be like a walk in the park. I can do this!

Excited about setting off on my new adventure, I bounce up the hill ahead and into the forest. I love walking, adore being surrounded by trees and like to meet new people. Despite the weather, this is fun!

I immediately like both Catarina and Brad, and hope that they feel the same. Even after only a few hours of their company, I am disappointed to learn that Catarina will shortly be leaving the group to walk ahead on her own for a few days before returning home. Brad is also planning to leave the group so that he can spend time walking alone. Just as I am making two new friends!

In the thick of the trees, we spot a totem pole next to the path ahead. No, not one – a group of them, all different heights. Next to them, there's a bench painted like a piano. A blue whale. A green lizard. What is this place? The others, having been on the trail for longer, recognise a stopping point for a food van. Unfortunately, the van has not yet arrived, so we munch on tangerines from our packs before continuing on our way.

By the time we drop down to San Juan de Ortega, my body is beginning to cry out for breakfast. Still like the new girl at school, I wait and watch. Do we all order food together or separately? Do we pay when we order or later? What food is on offer, and what does the group usually eat? It's all a mystery, and I don't like it much. I need to find my Camino mojo.

Hazel explains the procedure. Tortilla – a thick potato omelette – is on the menu, so we order that with tea and coffee and collect a stamp on our pilgrim passports.

As we wait for our food to arrive, a woman limps in, wincing with every step. Hazel slips into speaking French to find out what's wrong. This poor woman turned her ankle when she fell out of the top bunk a few days ago and is in quite a lot of pain.

I pull the bandage out of my first aid kit, and Catarina straps her ankle so she can continue walking.

The injured woman promises to visit a doctor when she gets to Burgos, as we fear that it is more than a sprain. It is another two days' walk to Burgos, but this does not seem to faze her.

By the time we leave the café, the rain and clouds have disappeared. It is promising to be a hot and sunny day.

Catarina is easy company. She is from Malmo in Sweden, a town I have enjoyed visiting. We make small talk and big talk as we walk. We cover families, politics and whether Malmo should become part of Denmark again now it has the bridge joining them. We comment on the countryside around us, and I find out why Catarina is walking the Camino. The depth of conversation and relationship seems to grow quickly. Is this an effect of being on the Camino?

Hazel suggests that we take a short detour to Atapuerca museum, as this is where the oldest human remains in the whole of Western Europe have been found. The museum is housed in a rusty hulk of a building that stands just outside the village. The gates are locked. No museum visit today!

We peer through the fence as we pass, and I get the impression that we are not missing much.

It is blisteringly hot as we walk into the village and find our hostel; I am glad that we are finishing our walk here today. The small stone building has a little bunkroom that is very different from last night's. The bunk beds are two high and sturdy, built into individual wooden cubicles, and there are ten beds in total in the room. Each has a curtain that gives us privacy as well as shade from any lights that others might use in the night.

There are only two showers – one for men and one for women – so it takes a while for us to wash ourselves and our clothes. There is nowhere to hang things up in the shower, so keeping clothes and valuables dry is a bit of a juggling act.

As I venture outside to hang my washing on the line, I notice a man a bit younger than me, sitting on the grass looking bereft. He is inspecting his feet, which are a mass of blisters and cracked skin.

It is only later that we find out that he is contemplating defeat. I say hello, but it is Hazel that does something that turns things round for him. She insists on looking at his feet. She will not take no for an answer. Between us and the various blister treatments we are carrying, we patch him up as best as we can. Hazel has already gained the trail name of 'Happy Feet' and I can see why. As well as helping others, hers are totally unblemished.

The village is little more than a scattering of low stone buildings with the odd tree or vine providing respite from the sun. Once we are all sorted, we head towards a bar, our new friend Lloyd hobbling along with us. Temperatures are soaring even higher now, so we rearrange some tables to allow us to sit in the shade.

Just as we finish, a man bursts out of the bar and shouts at us in Spanish.

Catarina and I look at each other. 'Well, if he's going to be like that, we'll go somewhere else.'

We stalk off, sure we'll find another bar. There are other bars in Atapuerca, but they are all closed. Half an hour later, we are back, with our tails between our legs. We hop between patches of shade as the sun moves across the sky. I choose food that I think does not need to go into the kitchen, in case the staff have taken umbrage at us. I am wrong – it is whisked away and reappears hot a few minutes later. I try not to think about the teenage summer I spent working in a kitchen when the staff would drop or spit on food if a customer upset them. We don't have a choice about where we eat, so I just have to suck it up.

Once the weight is off his feet, Lloyd turns out to be great company and a boost to our little group.

One other restaurant is open for dinner. The tables are available for pilgrims on a first come, first served basis, so we turn up early and queue, rather than risk eating in the same bar as earlier.

It is a 'pilgrims menu'. For only 13 Euros, we get a three-course meal with two choices for each course, wine and water. The pigs' cheeks have been slow-cooked in a rich sauce, so they are melt-in-the-mouth delicious; a good choice. The meal is filling, nutritious and the perfect way to end my first day on the Camino.

Despite my aching hip, I am optimistic that this will be a good trip.

Barely-Contained Fury

After the hills and forests of yesterday, we are walking in a different landscape today. We are leaving the bumpy foothills of the Pyrenees and heading towards the Meseta plain.

I am a little concerned about walking across the plain. I have heard that some pilgrims catch a bus across it because it's so boring. It will take two weeks for us to cross it – I hope they are wrong!

The hills are open and rolling, covered in green fields of ripening cereals. I have always been under the impression that they use a lot of pesticides and herbicides in Spain. I was wrong. Swathes of blood-red poppies stretch across the fields and a colourful mass of herbs and wildflowers line the path. Insects buzz around the flowers, alighting to drink the nectar or take a rest.

Walking is easy over this undulating landscape, and I contemplate how much I am enjoying the Camino already. This is such a perfect way to spend the day – walking through beautiful scenery in good company, with everything I need on my back. The sky is clear, yet I am on cloud nine.

We stop at a water fountain on the edge of the city of Burgos. As we approach, a man is shaking his head under the flow of water, cooling himself down. How refreshing that looks!

He heads back to his van, leaving the fountain to us. I lean towards the tap and hold my hands underneath it. Nothing. I touch the spout. Nothing. I look for a tap or switch. Nothing. Suddenly, the water starts to flow. I laugh and fill up my bottle with the cool liquid. It stops flowing before Catarina can fill hers. We start hunting for a tap again. We look high and low and round the side of the fountain. Nothing. It starts to flow again, apparently of its own accord, so Catarina quickly places her bottle under the tap. At exactly that moment, the flow stops.

What on earth is going on? Is there someone in one of the buildings here, playing with us by turning the fountain on and off? What a ridiculous thought, but there must be some explanation.

And so there is. Brad has noticed the button on the ground. It's him that is playing with us, stepping on and off the button. We all laugh at our confusion, applaud his observation skills and walk on.

It's not far before we pass a bar and can't resist stopping for a refreshing drink.

'Hi, Lloyd!' we call as he appears around the corner. Despite the state of his feet, he is walking faster than us and has caught us up after a later start. We regale the story of the magic fountain to him, laughing again at our farcical attempts to make it work.

The rest of the walk into Burgos is hard. The heat is amplified by the tall buildings and the pavement is unforgiving under our feet. We dive onto a path alongside the river, which at least has some tree shade. The black poplars seem to be shedding snow – their seed heads are covering everything with white fluff. I can't decide whether they look more like snow or some kind of nasty fungal growth.

Eventually, we leave the riverside and walk back into the built-up area, past an enormous statue of St James. The Camino de Santiago means 'the Way of St James' in English. James, one of the Twelve Apostles, preached Jesus' message of unconditional love and forgiveness here on the Iberian Peninsula. When he was martyred, his body was returned to what is now Santiago de Compostela. His relics purportedly reside in the cathedral, which is why this became a pilgrim route. There are images and statues of St James the pilgrim all along the route, but this one must be the most fragrant – it is covered in jasmine. The flowers are open, the scent is wafting around the pavement nearby, and the statue is abuzz with insects. We feast on the sight and scent of it before continuing our own pilgrimage into the city centre, where we are staying tonight.

Pilgrims of old would not have smelt freshly fragrant like the statue. I consider myself very lucky to be able to have a shower and wash my clothes every evening wherever we are staying. Hand-washing clothes might not be as effective as machine-washing them but does at least keep the worst of the pong at bay.

I did not plan to attend church while walking. I am not a Christian and was concerned it would feel hypocritical. However, I have changed my mind. If I was on a pilgrimage in Japan, I would go to the temples there, so why not here? There is a big pilgrim mass at the cathedral tonight that we have all decided to attend together.

The cathedral building is designed to impress. It is tall and imposing, with fancy Gothic stonework soaring up to the heavens. We arrive at the main entrance a few minutes before the service is due to start. The service takes place in a side chapel, and a barrier stops pilgrims from entering the main body of the church. Surely churches should be public spaces, especially along a busy pilgrim route?

When we are eventually allowed into the side chapel, I am taken aback by what I see. First, my eyes are drawn to the glinting of the statuary on the wall behind the altar. All that gold when there is so much poverty and starvation in the world.

The domed ceiling is plastered with cherub statuettes and other ornamentation in dull reds and blues on a creamy background. I begin to feel a little nauseous. I am by nature a bit of a minimalist and like to keep things simple. This level of opulence really does not sit well with me.

Things worsen as I pay more attention to the gold statuary. This is a Christian church, which is theoretically founded on the tenet of love. This is where people come for a regular reminder of how to behave in line with their values. And this is also where there are statues of dark-skinned people serving white people, of St James on a white horse, whipping two Arabic-looking men who are on the floor. St James the Pilgrim was appropriated by the church and turned into St James the Slayer of the Moors when driving the Moors out of Spain. This iconography remains, giving the clear message that white people are superior and that it is acceptable to do anything in the name of religion. The opulence suggests that concentration of wealth is good.

As I study the scene in front of me, I can feel my anger growing. Heat rises from my feet to the top of my head in an almost comical way. It feels like the top of my head might explode, Tom and Jerry-style. This is so far from the message of love that I associate with Christianity that I cannot stay any longer. As soon as I can without disrupting the whole congregation, I leave, fuming.

I stride around the square, trying to burn off some of the fury. It doesn't work, so I sit on a bench, close my eyes and focus on breathing. By the time the service has finished, I have calmed down but remain upset. How can I continue on a pilgrimage to Santiago when Santiago (St James) is portrayed as someone behaving like that?

Another Face of the Catholic Church

The heat and the thoughts jostling around in my head, combined with an aching hip, make for a bad night's sleep. This is not aided by the 5.15 a.m. wake-up call!

There is something special about walking before dawn. A full moon is shining over Burgos as we creep out, heading west. There is silence, except for a few birds and the rustle of clothes as pilgrims pour from the city, hoping to get some miles under their belts before the heat from the sun becomes overpowering.

Scallop shells marking the route of the Camino are set into the ground. Two-dimensional metallic figures of pilgrims line the path, glinting in the moonlight. It is not difficult to find our way. Even if there wasn't a steady stream of pilgrims heading in one direction, there are plenty of waymarkers. The path is particularly busy this morning. Most pilgrims stop overnight in the cities as they pass, and it takes a while for them to disperse again.

I am ravenous as we approach the first village of the day. It is time for breakfast. I sit with the rucksacks while the others go in to order. Everything we need for the Camino is in these bags, so I figure it's a good idea to keep an eye on them. The risk of theft may be small, but it would be pretty disruptive if it did happen.

I pull my knees up under my chin, huddling under my blanket. It is cooler here than in the city – a morning chill still hangs in the air. No doubt I will warm up with some tea and tortilla inside me, and it won't be long before we are walking again.

I spent the morning with Catarina, who will be leaving us later today. Even though we have only known each other for a couple of days, I will miss her. I have enjoyed her company and conversation.

We all hug when she departs. I wish her well in her deliberations and her life when she returns home.

The landscape here is magical. I expected it to be completely flat and uniform like a massive bowling green. Instead, it is bumpy, like rumpled silk. I understand something of the geological forces that have shaped the British landscape but not this. What has created such an effect?

Whatever it is, it feels wondrous. Once we are out on the plain, no navigation is needed – the wide, easy-going path just winds ahead into the distance. The wheat fields on each side of the path are a patchwork of colour from green to shimmering gold. Along the field margins and the path, there is an explosion of wild flowers, with the accompanying clouds of insects and butterflies buzzing around them. The chequerboard wings of the marbled white butterflies mix with others I don't recognise in striking shades of yellow, orange and vibrant blue. Birdsong fills the air, and an occasional cuckoo pierces the soundscape with its two-tone call.

As we are leaving Rabé de las Calzadas, I notice a nun ahead, beckoning the walkers in front of us into her church. After last night's experience, I am not inclined to go in. But the nun looks so crestfallen when the group in front of us ignores her, that I stop. I know that Hazel would like to go into churches when they are open, so I wait for her and we all troop inside.

It is a simple chapel, except for the decoration behind the altar. Although it is nowhere near as bad as the one in Burgos cathedral, it is still ostentatious and makes me recoil. The nun introduces herself as Teresa. She emanates love and concern for us as pilgrims. She stamps our pilgrim passports and hands us each a pendant to carry on our journey, with a prayer. Hazel puts hers around her neck, but I am not comfortable with that; I tuck mine into my rucksack instead. I remain unconvinced about the Catholic church and anyone or anything that represents it.

Teresa waves us over to the visitors' book. She asks us to share our reasons for walking the Camino. I wander round the church, feigning interest while the others write in the book. Eventually, I decide it would be churlish not to write in it myself. Hazel and Frank have settled onto a pew at the back of the church and Brad is heading towards the door.

I am not sure what to write, so peruse the notes that others have written. I flick through the book and read the first one I see in English. My heart lurches as I read the pilgrim's words of grief. Although the book is in a public place, I feel as though I have just read something that was not for my eyes. I quickly flick back to today's pages and leave my own message about how Teresa exemplifies the spirit of fellowship.

I join Hazel and Frank on the pew. They are sitting in silence with tears rolling down their faces. I do not need to ask why; I can guess. Being here, in this little church, with Teresa looking over us, we have a moment to reflect. I think about what I have just read and the tears flow for me too, feeling that person's pain and wishing them well.

Teresa sees what is happening. She dashes to the front of the church and turns the music off. She brings out her mobile phone and hands it to me. I watch musicians play the most beautiful song. The sound swirls around and seems to permeate me. At the end of the song, I hand her phone back and thank her. She passes me a packet of tissues and leaves me to my thoughts and tears.

As we depart, Teresa tells us that she will hold us in her heart and her thoughts all the way to Santiago. She holds my hands and then accepts a hug. I may not wear the pendant, but I will certainly hold the love that Teresa has shared with us in my heart. This, to me, is exactly what the Christian church and faith are all about. The Catholic church has redeemed itself. A little.

For a while, I walk in silence, deep in my thoughts, contemplating life and enjoying my surroundings. Is this where my Camino has really started?

Mercury Rising

The view down to the village ahead stops me in my tracks. The old stone buildings sit in a wide depression, surrounded by a scattering of trees; rare in these parts. I drink in the different hues of gold that adorn the fields. The wide white path draws my eye into the heart of the village. The heat is beginning to feel oppressive under the washed-out blue of the cloudless sky, but I could walk through this landscape forever. My heart is singing.

'That's our destination for the day – Hornillos del Camino.'

My heart sinks. I am not ready to stop walking yet. I have miles left in my legs. And need miles more contemplation time.

I have a thumping headache that has been following me all day despite my attempts to drink the plain dry. Walking is providing me with a distraction; I have no desire to stop here. But, I am walking with a group, so I do. At least, I think, it will give me a chance to rest.

The trees stop before we reach the settlement. The heat is reflecting from the stone buildings that straddle the narrow road through the village, intensified as it has nowhere to go. While the others sit in a pool set up at the hostel to cool pilgrims down, I seek the shade of a tree for some quiet contemplation.

I walk the length of the village, my internal temperature steadily rising and my headache steadily worsening. The only tree in the whole village is in a private garden. Instead, I have to make do with building shade. It is better than nothing, but nowhere near as cool or refreshing as tree shade. It is cooler here than in the direct sun, but my core temperature is still rising.

Tonight's dinner is communal, which means that I'm going to have to be sociable. I am a strong introvert, so always find occasions like that difficult. When I am overheated and have a mad axeman trying to break out through my skull, that difficulty is magnified many times over.

'Can I pretend to be mute?' I ask my Camino family, only partially in jest.

'No!'

Dinner is not as much of a trial as I feared, but sleeping is.

I am pleased, at least, that we have a room with just the four of us in. Lloyd joined us for lunch but is not staying with us tonight.

The room is stifling and I have a top bunk. We have been given a mobile air conditioning unit, but it is having no impact at all. I am lying in my bunk, trying to relax before lights out when I lose my patience.

I am beside myself. My head hurts, and I am far too hot. It is time to move my mattress to the floor. The ladder of the bunk-bed slips as I climb down. I shake it in frustration, startling my room mates as it rattles loudly. I have lost my cool, literally and figuratively!

I eventually manage to squeeze the mattress into a space on the floor and go for a cold shower. I do not dry myself, in the hope that evaporative cooling will drop my temperature. It has no discernible effect, and I am dry within a few seconds.

If I can't cool myself down, I need to calm myself down. I grab my earphones, play some soothing music and close my eyes.

The night is long and fragmented. All the dorm doors are open to try to create a cooling draught through the building. The hallway light is controlled by a movement sensor, so every time someone gets up to go to the bathroom, the light shines directly in my face. While in the bathroom, it switches off. When they leave the bathroom, it blinds me again. This strobe effect continues all night. And just as it's cooling down enough to have a chance of some sleep, it is time to start walking again.

Cooler

Heat is still radiating from the village buildings as we walk through it in the dark. There is a noticeable drop in temperature as we leave the stone behind. Perhaps I should have slept outside the village last night, on the ground under a tree.

My headache persists until I have my first cup of tea of the day, when it disappears in an instant. I realise that yesterday, I did not drink tea at all. Maybe I'm addicted to it. I leave this thought in the back of my mind as I enjoy the flavour and reassurance that a lovely hot cup of tea delivers, even when the weather is equally as hot. If I am addicted, then now is not the time to go cold turkey.

The beauty of the plain continues for mile after mile. Today, the wildflowers have changed in nature. There is a lot of chamomile alongside the path. The white daisy-like flowers are covered in little beetles. Black and red moths, similar to our cinnabar moth but with a different pattern, sit alongside. Despite the lack of sleep last night and the searing heat today, I have a spring in my step.

Nevertheless, I am pleased to reach our destination for the day – Castrojeriz, a small town built on a hill that's topped by a castle. The heat is suffocating, so we dive into the first bar we see for some cool drinks and ham sandwiches. Lloyd whips a heavy glass jar of Colman's mustard out of his pack.

'This'll spice it up a bit!'

I laugh. All that unnecessary weight!

'Any meal can be improved with some mustard. I always carry a jar with me.'

Somewhat revived by our break and time spent in the shade, we walk through the town to our accommodation. I would like to visit the castle, but this heat is sapping all my energy. I cannot contemplate walking to the top of a shadeless hill in this.

We arrange for Lloyd to join us for the communal dinner at the hostel tonight. I am not looking forward to trying to sleep in a big, overheated dorm.

They say that the Camino provides, and it does this evening. We are shown to a room for just the four of us, and it has working air conditioning. We rearrange the beds so they are all in the cool draught and relax.

At dinner, we hear that the big dorm is stifling. We all keep schtum about our air conditioning – we don't want to gloat.

Dinner is over and my introverted self has had enough of company for now. I head back to the room to spend some time alone before lights out and the promise of a good night's sleep.

A Stormy Night

The air conditioning stopped working sometime during the night, but I didn't notice at all – it was not the heat that kept me awake. It was my legs. They were incredibly restless, compelling me to keep moving all night. I hope I didn't keep the others awake. It feels as though I don't fit in my skin, and I have an irresistible urge to move my limbs. It was only a couple of years ago that I discovered this can be a sign of iron deficiency.

I kick myself when I realise that I forgot to take my iron tablet last night. Such a seemingly small thing means that I am starting another day drained and not at my best. I swallow one with breakfast and set a daily reminder on my phone.

Breakfast at the hostel is a poor affair. It's barely edible and provides little nutrition for the day ahead. As I load my plate into the dishwasher, I receive an electric shock and whip my hand away from the offending machine. A member of staff strides over, scowling at me and points to my feet. She reprimands me for not wearing shoes to earth myself. I scowl back, perplexed at her attitude.

It is still early – and dark – as we leave the hostel. It seems to have rained during the night – there are puddles underfoot, which are tricky to avoid by moonlight. We dance our way along the valley floor, then slog up a long slope onto a ridge. The view back over Castrojeriz is stunning. It is just light enough to see the hill with the castle on it rising behind the village, in an otherwise flat valley. A steep escarpment frames each side of the long, wide valley.

At the far side of the ridge, the Meseta plain stretches off into the distance. I follow the line of our path as it winds away to its vanishing point. Another smile lights up my face. What a view! And I get to spend the day walking across it. Wow!

As the sun rises, the temperature follows. A dampened travel towel around my neck helps to keep me cool. The walking is not trying. The terrain is easy and little navigation is needed. We arrive at our hostel in Boadilla del Camino quickly after what feels like another short day of walking.

Another stone village, this one is built around the church and square to one side, rather than along a narrow main street. The hostel forms one side of the square. I hope this will reduce the urban heat island effect of buildings close to each other, reflecting the heat back and forth.

After a cooling drink in the air-conditioned bar, we head to the dorm where there are twenty or so beds set out in two rows. It is in the roof space of a modern building, overlooking the squat old church. It is warm, but the breeze through the skylights makes it comfortable. Storks are nesting on the church roof, rattling their beaks. I lie on my bed contemplating life, listening and smiling to myself. I have never heard that sound before.

The church is open, so we take a quick look round before dinner. The usual ostentatious gold screen adorns the wall behind the altar. In contrast, a simple but beautifully carved 14th-century stone font sits on a short plinth at the opposite end of the church. The medieval tower in the village square is more ornate, yet somehow complements the very plain stonework of the church.

There's an old tank in the village, with a sign warning that the water is not potable. A modern tap alongside provides cool fresh water for my bottle. Glooping noises reverberate from the old stone tank. Something is in there, but I can't identify what. Or maybe it's in the reeds nearby. The sound seems to move around. I peer this way and that, trying to place it – both in space and in my memory. My imagination is fired up. Is it a weird bird call, a gloop monster, or just frogs? I plump for the latter, although the idea of monsters is now firmly planted in my mind. Perhaps I have had too much sun today!

The lentil dinner is delicious, although I do worry about the effect that the lentils might have on twenty of us, all sharing a room! It is not that, but a storm that scuppers a good night's sleep this time. The room is bearably warm as we head to bed, but at lights-out time, the owner bustles in and closes all the windows, even the vents.

'There's a storm coming. You cannot open the windows.'

The wind whips around the roof and the temperature immediately soars, as though the room has been dunked into hot magma. A pleasantly warm room has become stifling in just a few minutes. I understand why the windows need to be closed, but this heat is intolerable.

I walk to the bathroom and douse myself with water. I cover myself with a wet towel to try to cool down. Once again, it dries almost instantly, with no discernible effect. Once again, I don't know what to do with myself.

Eventually, the wind subsides and I open all the windows I can reach. Slowly, like a glacier wending its way down a mountain, the room starts to cool, and I drift off to sleep.

'What on earth?' I frown, blinking in the light. A headtorch is shining right in my face. It does not last for long; the owner turns on the lamp above his bed instead, then walks the whole length of the dorm to the bathroom, leaving the light on. When he returns, he starts to pack, slowly, meticulously and noisily.

It's 3 a.m. I have barely slept for two hours. By 4.30, we have all had enough.

'We may as well get up ourselves.'

Sleep

As we wander across the square, I wonder whether sleep deprivation is part of the reason that the Camino is such a successful pilgrimage. Perhaps pilgrims see visions as a result...

And indeed, my brain offers me a vision as we walk to the drinking fountain to refill our bottles. The gloop monsters are there again. I fight the urge to run.

'It's just frogs, Julia.'

Probably, but I have never heard frogs anywhere else that sound like that!

An easy walk for a few kilometres leads us to breakfast. The hostel has a delightfully cool and shady garden and serves the best breakfast yet. Silky smooth scrambled eggs make a welcome change to the usual chunky tortilla. Another moonlit walk and a delicious breakfast in a beautiful garden have revived me, ready for the long walk ahead.

My Camino family met a young Danish man called Emil before I joined them. After having had a few rest days in the cities, he has caught us up. I walk with him for a few kilometres, chatting comfortably. When I was his age, I found walking intensely boring – it was far too slow for my liking. When he set off to walk the Camino, he was worried that he might feel the same way. He doesn't. He tells me that he has mainly walked on his own, although he enjoys walking with other people for a while sometimes too. He is good company, and I hope we will bump into him again.

The landscape is different today, wetter. The path follows watercourses for much of the day. Frogs call in a distinctly different language than they do at home. Thin lines of open water snake through the duckweed. They are too small and close together to be duck trails. Perhaps they have been left by frogs. Unless, of course, there really are (miniature) monsters lurking!

Tonight, we are staying in a convent in Carrión de Los Condes. I find what I think is the pilgrim entrance in the high metal gate and try the handle. It gives, leading into a spacious courtyard. We cross to the reception area – a large room with a solitary table standing right in the middle, flanked by two nuns. One remains at the desk, while the other shows us to our room. Thankfully, the beds are not bunks, and there are four under the open windows. We grab these, hoping to benefit from any cool night air as it descends.

The gates of the compound are locked overnight; they take their curfew seriously here. I have heard horror stories of people being locked into the buildings they are staying in, but at least this one has a large courtyard. If there is a fire, we will be able to retreat some distance from the building.

Carrión is a larger town that gives the impression of having a degree of wealth and importance. We eat in the spacious town square, joined by Emil and some others. One of the young women looks at Frank and proclaims:

'You have the most beautiful blue eyes!'

We laugh, causing her to blush furiously.

'You're right,' I say, hoping to spare her a little embarrassment. 'He does.'

Frank is a hit with most people he meets. I think that is something to do with his easy smile and twinkling blue eyes. With this, he somehow exudes a sense of laid-back fun. From this moment on, Frank's trail name becomes 'Ole Blue Eyes'.

I leave the group to explore the town, looking for a view of a magnificent building on a bluff that I have seen on a postcard. I do not find the view but recharge on my own in a garden by the river. Thunder gently rumbles through the clouds overhead, but it doesn't feel threatening. Until that is, a crack of lightning whips through the air and the heavens open. I run to the nearest shelter, a very shallow doorway, and squeeze myself flat against the door to avoid a drenching.

A few minutes later, the rain has subsided so I make a dash for it across the road to some more substantial shelter, then back to the convent, where I meet Jae Eun, a Korean woman who is sharing our dorm.

At 10 p.m., it is lights-out time. A nun walks into the room and switches off the light, even though Hazel is still sorting things out on her bed. We negotiate with the nun and promise we will turn the light out soon if she allows us a few more minutes to settle down. She agrees and leaves us to it.

The cool post-storm air does indeed blow across us during the night. I realise just as I drift off that my hip has stopped hurting. Walking every day has eased the pain as I hoped it would. I sleep like a baby.

Turning Point

The Meseta rolls on. Day after day, we walk through the fresh, moonlit morning and the gentle golden light of sunrise, and then stop before the heat of the day becomes too ferocious. We are walking into our shadows, always heading west.

We eat together, meet new friends, talk, think and listen.

The wildlife continues to enchant and delight. At dawn, salamanders crawl onto the path to bask. We admire them and get close to one with our cameras. Eventually, we realise it is probably terrified, but not warm enough yet to be able to run away. We move it into the sun at the side of the path.

As if to prove that we are up with the larks, they are the first birds to break the morning silence. At one point, there is a flock of them, almost deafening with their insistent 'space invaders' tweeting as we pass.

Every day, a cuckoo continues to call, as though it is following us west. Storks nest precariously on all sorts of improbable ledges and gradients. Butterflies adorn the herbs and flowers on the verges, creating a shimmering mirage alongside the path.

Most mornings, Lloyd gets up and sets off later than us. When he catches up, we walk together for the rest of the day. He is fun to have around, and he's having more fun himself now his feet are beginning to heal.

One day we arrive at a hostel to find that we have been allocated a separate suite. Two rooms – three beds in one and a double in the other. It is easy sharing with people we know well by now. I relax far more than I ever do in a bigger dorm. I sleep well. This stay marks a turning point. By unspoken agreement, we start to plan overnight stops in smaller dorms with just our Camino family, when we can.

Halfway

On the approach to Sahagún, the path veers off under some tall trees. The waymarker is topped with a pair of boots, filled with soil and planted with flowers. A small bridge leads to a chapel, some shady picnic tables and an arch.

This is the halfway point for pilgrims who started walking in St-Jean-Pied-de-Port. For the others in my Camino family, this is an important point. If you can walk half the distance, you can walk the other half, too. There are smiles all round and a lightness of step as we cover the next few hundred metres into the town.

We head to the Iglesia de la Trinidad for the others to pick up certificates marking their achievement. As we sit outside a café with drinks, I wonder what the second half of our journey will bring.

Mountains Loom

After Sahagún, things change. It's subtle, but I feel it. Clouds are creating wondrous shapes in the sky and giving it a deeper, richer hue. We have not heard any cuckoos for a couple of days, but skylarks are becoming more common. Occasionally we see deer in the fields, foraging in the early morning light.

Until now, none of the fields of sunflowers has been in bloom. Here, there is one field in its full glory. Brown faces skirted with joyful yellow petals look towards us, as if in greeting. How can you not be glad when looking at a field of golden sunflowers?

Brad interrupts my reverie. 'You know, on the first day you joined us, you reminded me of Snow White in the film. She throws opens the window and cheerfully greets the morning, the trees, the birds and the sky. I really wasn't sure I was going to be able to cope with you bouncing around and being so positive all the time. And you haven't stopped! Here we are, weeks later, and you're still greeting the skylarks, deer and sunflowers.

'But I've come to like that about you. I'm glad we met. I think your trail name should be Snow Light – a combination of

Snow White and your obsession with keeping the weight of your rucksack down.'

I think about this for a few moments. Snow Light. I like it.

'OK, Snow Light it is.'

Mountains appear in the distance to the north. As the days progress, they seem to curve round until we are heading directly towards them.

After two weeks of walking across the plain, we are not mountain-fit. How will our legs manage when they have hills to climb again? I'm not sure, but I realise that every pilgrim must feel the same – and most make it through, so no doubt we will too.

It is midsummer and we continue to walk, day after day. One morning, with our shadows still long, we notice a faint rainbow ahead. A sprinkler is watering the path. It is arcing to and fro, and we realise that if we time it just right, we can run past without getting wet. Frank and Brad are in front. Hazel and I watch and learn. They make it through unscathed, so it's our turn. As the water arcs away from us, we follow, jumping over puddles. As it crosses from the path into the field, we run, making the most of the few seconds before it returns.

It doesn't matter if we get wet. We are, after all, walking through a heatwave, but it is a fun game to punctuate the day, a game that we all win.

In places, the track is stony, the sort of surface you could easily turn an ankle on. The others tell me they are having to concentrate to avoid hurting themselves. For some reason, I don't find it particularly difficult. They can also feel the stones through the soles of their shoes, as their shoes have two weeks more wear than mine. I am glad to have well-padded soles, especially as so much of the route is on hard ground.

On one particularly quiet and isolated stretch of path, a couple of cars roll down the track towards us and turn off just before they reach us. They pull to a stop and the men who are driving stay inside and watch as we pass. Hazel and I glance at each other. We do not need to say it out loud; if either of us had been walking on our own, we would have been concerned about our safety at this point. But, as we are in a group, we feel safer. Nevertheless, we keep an eye on them until they drive away.

Feeling Unsafe

We have started to book smaller rooms when we can, but for tonight, we couldn't. We are in the only hostel with space available, in a dorm with about forty beds in it. The entrance to the accommodation is directly from a bar, and somehow this combination of size and access makes it feel unsafe.

Lloyd has booked into a hotel as his wife will be joining us later tonight. It's their wedding anniversary tomorrow, so she will be with us for a few days.

That leaves four of us in the big dorm. We are spread out, as there aren't four beds together. We watch our phones as they charge. I tie my rucksack to the bed. This would not stop anyone determined to steal it but makes it harder to swipe surreptitiously. When we leave to explore the town, we carry our valuables and anything else we can't live without.

Mansilla de las Mulas is a fortified town from the 13th century, with a lot of the walls intact. As we are admiring one of the gates, a local man calls us over and excitedly dashes round the town giving us a whistle-stop tour of the churches and squares. He leaves us at a painted passageway leading to a sally port – a small door to the walled enclosure. I have only seen these in castles before and was not aware that you find them in town walls too. Our guide explains that he must get back to work, ducks into a nearby alley and disappears, leaving us to complete our tour.

Lloyd's wife has been delayed, so when she arrives after dinner, I say hello and then head straight to bed. All my senses are on high alert in this huge dorm. Sleep evades me until the rest of my Camino family return. Their presence is soothing and eventually, with one eye half open, sleep descends.

Dog Attack

Everything in Spain seems a little less controlled than at home. The houses are less well-maintained, and the gardens less manicured. The field and path margins are brimming with wildflowers. And the dogs are more likely to be untethered.

I adore the sections of the path where you can see it ribboning off ahead for miles across the landscape. Even when we're walking on a tarmac road, there's something rather magical about the effect.

There is one small group of pilgrims on the road ahead. They are walking towards a couple of unleashed dogs that watch as they approach. It seems that the corner where the dogs are prowling is their territory and the pilgrims are marching straight into it. They haven't seen the dogs yet and we are too far away to warn them. They are walking in a straggle, with space between chatting pairs. As the first pilgrims cross an invisible line, the dogs run towards them and start snapping at their legs. The pilgrims are hassled like this until they have passed through the dogs' territory. The dogs strut back to their corner, lie down and watch the stretch of road we are about to walk along.

We stop for a conflab. We need a strategy for passing these dogs. We decide to walk in a close-knit group. Those with poles slip their wrists from the straps and remove the rubber ferrules from the tips, so they can be used as a deterrent if need be. Those of us without are bundled into the middle of the group, surrounded by people with poles. We decide that it is best to walk confidently and briskly, staying together and ignoring the dogs as best we can, while keeping a close eye on them.

Perhaps I should have brought some poles with me after all. Until now, I have been happy not to have any. Now, I'm not so sure.

As we near the dogs, my heart starts to race. A little frisson of excitement that reminds me that I am alive – and not invincible. As we approach, the dogs watch us but remain lying on the far side of the corner.

We pass without incident. Perhaps they have had their fill of hassling pilgrims for today. We relax. I can't resist turning to watch as the next group nears the corner. Will the dogs remain relaxed with them? No. The dogs were up and growling, darting close to their legs and back out again. That group of pilgrims had also been spread out along the road. Perhaps our tight formation and use of poles were enough to psyche the dogs out as we passed.

Whatever the truth of the matter, I am relieved – and I hope that's the last we'll see of aggressive dogs.

Is it All Over?

The approach to the city of León is as noisy and busy as expected, until the route ducks off to one side into a pedestrian area. A short stretch of the city wall comes into view, formed from large pebbles set into mortar. As we approach, I realise it is two walls, not one, with a wide walkway between giving a clear view of the structure for some distance. The outer wall is around twice the height of a person and has a stone walkway behind it for soldiers. Anyone who successfully assailed the outer wall would then be faced with the inner one, rising twice as high. Both have crenellations – the distinctive shape of battlements the world over. What a formidable fortification!

The sky is darkening as we near the city centre, threatening rain. My heart skips a beat when I spot a building on the far side of a square. It is just a little bit offbeat. The stone façade is not completely smooth like those of the other buildings and the stone blocks are not uniform in size. The turrets in each corner are small in diameter with unnecessarily tall witch's-hat roofs. Even the ridgeline of the roof is textured, not smooth. I would like to take a closer look, but we are on a mission to find our accommodation before the rain starts and I have some jobs to get done before I can explore.

Mike and I are buying a house and I need to get some paperwork done now I'm in a city. I spend a few hours sorting things out while most of the others tour the city and visit the cathedral. We are spread out tonight – Hazel and I are sharing a double and Frank and Brad have a room each. It's Lloyd and Sarah's wedding anniversary, so they have a hotel room booked a couple of streets away.

Brad has spent the afternoon in his room and texts me just as I finish the paperwork. Do I want to go to see the fabulous building we spotted on the way in? He has read that it was designed by Gaudí, famous for his buildings in Barcelona. We head out together. First stop, the hiking shop to pick up some bits for Brad, then on to the square in front of the building.

As we approach, the heavens open. I jump a few puddles, then another. Pain slices through my calf, stopping me dead. It feels like the muscle has become unattached at one end and rolled up under my knee. I cannot put weight on my right leg. I clench my teeth and try not to cry as Brad helps me to a bench inside the building. I massage my leg, ever optimistic that something so simple will have a positive effect. It doesn't. We consult the internet and conclude that I have torn my calf muscle. If that's the case, it will take six to eight weeks to heal.

Is my Camino over?

I quickly push the thought aside – that won't help right now. It's time to get practical. First things first, I need to get back to the hotel to cool and elevate my leg and take some anti-inflammatories.

With Brad's help, I make it down the steps back into the square and try to take a step forwards. I cry out involuntarily. Walking is impossible.

'It's OK, Julia. You're light, I'll carry you back to the hotel.'

It doesn't take Brad long to find out that I'm heavier than I look. Nevertheless, he manages to get me back to the hotel in one piece. I use the bannister to haul myself up the stairs, one step at a time. The pain is excruciating. Why does our room have to be on the second floor?

Brad leaves me when I reach the safety of my room. There is nothing more he can to do help me. He may as well join the others for dinner.

My leg doesn't feel too bad when it's propped up against the wall. Perhaps it's not as bad as I thought. I get up to use the bathroom. Oh my goodness, that hurts! Self-pity washes over me for a while. It's time to call Mike. I don't want to worry him, but he's the only person I want to talk to. I know he'll cheer me up and help me to move from self-pity into a more positive state of mind.

And it works. We talk about all the ways I could continue if I can't walk. A bicycle, perhaps? An electric scooter? A sedan chair? I find myself laughing and plotting for a more favourable future. I resolve to seek medical help in the morning if I need to and to continue with the group for a few days by taxi while I assess the situation further.

Pepe

I sleep well, despite the pain and the noise from a local fiesta. Hazel sneaks in late, having joined in some of the fun, and sneaks out again early to start walking. By the time I get up, I can take a small step forward on one leg. Hazel has left me her walking poles, so I use them to get to the pharmacy for anti-inflammatories and painkillers, one tiny step at a time. The poles are so useful that I buy a pair for myself on the way back to the hotel.

If you look hard enough, there's always a silver lining. Today, it is having the opportunity to spend some time with Lloyd's wife, Sarah. We share a taxi to the hostel and sit in the garden, chatting.

A message pings into Sarah's phone. 'They're almost here. I think I'll walk out to meet them.'

'Me too.' My leg is improving; I think I might be able to shuffle to the edge of the village, especially if Sarah is with me to help if needed.

I stand up on my good leg, grab my walking poles and hop down the steps. Hopping is not a good long-distance option, so once at the bottom, I start to walk. One tiny step forward onto my right leg, weight on the walking poles. Bring my left leg forward to meet it. Relax. I can barely step forward at all on my left leg; it is agony pushing off from my right foot. I bring the right foot to join it. 20cm at a time. Step, join. Wait, relax. Step, join. Repeat.

It is slow progress. About 50m down the road, there is a Camino waymarker low enough to sit on.

'I think you should stop here,' Sarah says. I agree and perch on the sign, using my walking poles to balance. I watch Sarah continue down the road to meet with the group. I might not have got far, but my heart is thumping in my chest. It's only a few metres, but that's a few metres further than I thought would be possible yesterday. I beam as I join the others to return to the hostel.

That afternoon, I manage to walk, albeit painfully slowly, to a bar for lunch and a drink.

Back at the hostel, we have dinner and socialise with other pilgrims. There is little phone signal here, so the hostel staff offer to call a taxi for Sarah to take her back to the airport, and me to our next stop. Hopefully, the rest of my Camino will not be by car!

When it comes to ordering a taxi in the morning, the hostel owner, who was grumpy last night, still is.

'Why are you ordering two separate taxis?'

'Because my friend is flying home today and I am injured, so I'm travelling on to meet the others at the end of their walk today.'

One of his staff starts to interpret for us.

'Pepe used to be a massage therapist. He could help you.'

Seeing the indecision on my face, she continues. 'He is well known locally as a healer. He won't hurt you.'

One more moment of indecision, until I realise that I have nothing to lose. I can't travel by taxi forever and really do want to continue walking.

I sit in the dining room and Pepe lifts my leg onto his knee. I can feel his nails scrape against and pinch my skin as he runs his hands down the back of my calf muscle.

'You haven't torn your calf muscle. Your tendons have crossed. I will straighten them out for you.'

He runs his hands down my calf again, then pulls his hand back as though he has received an enormous electric shock.

'Have I hurt him?' I ask the interpreter, worried.

The two talk for a moment before she answers. 'No. He says that the pain has transferred from you to him. It means that you are healed. You can walk now.'

Really? Could it possibly be as simple as that? I stand up and try to walk. No, it isn't as simple as that. I cry out in pain and clutch my leg.

'He says your leg only hurts now because you are expecting it to. You can walk normally.'

I try again. It is improved, although I cannot take a full stride.

The taxi takes me to the next place we have booked to stay. I arrive a few hours earlier than check-in, but the owners take pity on me. The room I am sharing with Hazel is ready, so they are happy for me to use it. I peel back the covers on the bed, crawl in and sleep. Hours later when I surface, I walk to the bathroom carefully but unaided. I can step forward on both feet, as long as my pace is short enough.

'Wow! Pepe really is a healer,' I think as I contemplate walking out of the village to meet the others.

'I can walk. My Camino isn't over!' Tears spring to my eyes as the realisation dawns.

Slowly, slowly, I walk down the street, one foot in front of the other, to join the Camino and start to walk it in reverse, leaving the village. A group of pilgrims is walking down the path ahead. The gaits are familiar. It's my Camino family! They are earlier than expected. I will not get to walk far today, but maybe that's a good thing.

On the way back into the village, a couple of school children are selling decorated scallop shells. I am feeling optimistic, like a real pilgrim again. I buy a shell to hang from my pack, proud to announce my pilgrim status to the world. The shell does not remain with me for the rest of the journey, but for now, it symbolises something important. I am a pilgrim and I will finish my pilgrim's journey. I am grateful to Pepe, the healer, and am reminded once again that you should never judge a book by its (grumpy) cover.

Back on Track

There is nothing to do in the village except eat and drink, so that is how we spend the rest of the day. Lloyd buys us each a hard-boiled egg stuffed with tuna. They are served with just a cocktail stick to eat with. We roll around laughing, watching each other try to negotiate such a tricky task.

A message arrives on my phone: Our flight home has been cancelled. Hazel, Frank and I are travelling together, so all three of us are stranded. We decide that today is a day for jollity, so we push the problem to one side and focus on having some fun.

Apparently, drinking alcohol impairs the healing process, so no more for me on this trip. Thankfully, most bars serve alcohol-free beer. The rest of the group is topping up their natural ebullience with the normal variety. Lloyd heads back to the bar to get another round in and returns with a plate of lobster paella that he has blagged from a birthday celebration inside. We laugh and tuck in. A few minutes later, the bar owner appears with the rest of the left-over paella. It is a veritable feast that fits our jubilant mood perfectly.

'¡Felicidades!' Happy Birthday!

Given the generally bubbly atmosphere, I am extremely careful on the short walk back to the hostel, while also trying to race the others to one of the two hammocks! They respect my efforts and let me win, allowing me time to sleep again, this time while swinging in the breeze.

The communal meal is delicious, and just us with one other guest. Our mood remains buoyant, aided by our fellow pilgrim.

After a good night's sleep, I ship my bag and eat breakfast at the hostel. Even here, where the food was so good last night, the breakfast is not great. It is not a meal designed to give pilgrims energy for the day!

I am so heartened by yesterday's progress that I am going to try to walk 10km today. We have hatched a plan that involves me catching a taxi to Astorga, and then walking to our destination. If I have trouble on the way, the group will catch me up and be able to help.

Astorga appears to be an interesting town, worth looking around. There is another Gaudí building here that I would love to see inside, but this is not a day for sightseeing; it is a day for walking.

Carefully, I set off through the town. It's strange walking on my own, but I love having this time to spend in my own thoughts and I know that my friends are following. It's a beautiful morning, and all the more so because I am back on the trail. At first, I am cautious with each step, but it's not long before I become more confident. Walking normally is no longer painful at all. Thank you, Pepe!

On the outskirts of town, I pop into the church at Homo Ecco. Most of the churches we have passed have been closed and locked. This is infuriating on such a popular pilgrimage route, so it's always a treat to find one open. I light a candle and send my best wishes out into the universe for various friends with issues they are dealing with; family, loss, a change of path. I sit and hold each in my heart for a few minutes before stamping my pilgrim passport and continuing on my way. I would like to do this in every church I pass, creating a ripple of love through the layers of the universe.

Lost in my thoughts, I leave the city behind. As the route switches from pavement to path, I concentrate on walking again, just to be careful on this new, less-even surface.

The countryside is beautiful and the warmth of the sun provides a welcome contrast to the cool breeze. The path is wide, a few metres away from the road. A patchwork of fields is punctuated by large areas of scrub pushing through the undergrowth and immature forestry plantations. The flat plain has turned into low rolling hills, rising into the mountains.

A police car cruises past a couple of times, the officers keeping an eye on this quiet stretch of path. There are no other pilgrims in sight, so although crime rates in Spain are low, the police presence is reassuring.

Men walk out from the villages and pick flowers and herbs to create a wild posy, presumably to give to their wives or sweethearts. I have never seen a man do this in Britain, and, anyway, we are discouraged from picking wildflowers. In Spain, though, there are fewer people and more flowers, and my smile broadens even further to see such a loving and simple gesture.

A labyrinth by the side of the path catches my attention. I take a few minutes to wander through it into the centre and back out again. Another moment for meditation.

Although the churches are often closed and therefore not available to sit in and think, lots of people have taken the time to leave small messages to encourage reflection as you walk. Graffiti about turning your lead into gold adorns signs. Stones have poems painted onto them. The word LOVE is spelt out in stones alongside the path. There are many reminders that this is no ordinary long-distance walk.

As I near the day's destination, I reflect on how special this route is. There is one concern gnawing at the back of my mind, though. I have not yet worked out what burden I will be leaving behind at the Iron Cross, only a few days away now.

Back in the Flow

After yesterday's success, I decide to walk with the group today. I hope this won't be pushing things too far. I loved walking on my own yesterday, but am ready for company again.

The walking is much trickier today – I'm so glad this is not my first day back on the trail! The path is less even, with more changes of direction. I pay close attention to each step so that I don't exceed my ability and undo all of Pepe's good work. There is still an occasional gasp of pain when I do something a bit more ambitious than I should, and a long step or a leap could set me back by days.

My bag is being shipped again so my leg is under less pressure. It is a hard day's walking, but I can't stop smiling. Only a few days ago, I thought my Camino might be over. The saying that the Camino provides is shown to be true once more – this time in the form of Pepe the healer.

The hills have loomed in the distance for days, conjuring images of Hobbit-style mountainous hardship, but the climb up is not as bad as I feared. Nevertheless, I am glad to arrive at

Foncebadon. My legs are a little wobbly, but there has not been anything too taxing to tackle.

We are up in the hills now and the Meseta feels like a distant memory already! The wide open landscapes of the plain made my heart sing, and now the lush green hills are having the same effect.

We are nearing the Iron Cross. We are high in the mountains and the heatwave of the plains has turned into the chill of the hills. Five of us have booked to stay together tonight, and when we are shown to our room in the hostel, there is only one other bed in the dorm.

'Only one extra bed. Hopefully, that means we will be on our own tonight.' I am not the only person finding dorm-life wearing.

Lloyd and I draw the short straws for a top bunk. I don't mind, but it's always a bit trickier to manoeuvre down the steps if you need to get up at night. After we have started to lay our things out, Lloyd notices that his bunk only has a barrier on one side.

Brad, who likes to be prepared for every eventuality – and whose weighty pack reflects this – whips out a length of paracord and ties it across the gap. It would not stop Lloyd from falling, but would at least alert him to being at the edge of the bed. Lloyd is reassured, although not totally happy.

Just as we are leaving for dinner, an Italian man appears, chewing an unlit cigar. He has been assigned the final bunk in our room. Despite our disappointment, we smile and welcome him, using Google Translate to communicate. We agree on a time for lights out and to get up in the morning so that we don't disturb each other, then head out.

As we are all preparing for sleep, we are given a start. We exchange wild-eyed stares. Italian Man has just got into bed. He is lying on his side, facing the room, and has immediately started to snore like a trooper. It's going to be a noisy night.

'Here, Julia, have my spare earplugs. I think you're going to need them tonight.'

The earplugs dull the noise a little, but even though I am on the other side of the room, his snores reverberate loudly, as if he is right next to me. Thank goodness he's not!

This is the night that we all need to sleep well. We have an early start in the morning, and an emotional day as we visit the Iron Cross. I'm not sure I sleep a single wink. The room is frigid and the cold easily penetrates the two blankets piled over me. The only respite from the snoring is when Italian Man gets up to go to the loo. There is ambient light in the room, but he switches his head torch on anyway and flashes the light into our eyes one by one as he navigates across the room to the bathroom.

He opens the door wide and then switches on the light, blinding the two of us closest to the door. A few minutes later, he repeats the manoeuvre when he returns, disturbing us all again. Eventually, one of us breaks.

'Turn your bloody head torch off!' Italian Man doesn't speak a word of English, but the tone is clear and the light clicks off.

Bliss!

A creak as he climbs back into his bunk is quickly followed by the continuation of the high-volume snoring. Sometimes, being a pilgrim does test your patience!

I lie awake in my bunk, trying to be still, waiting for morning to arrive.

This is likely to be an emotional day, as we all leave our burdens at the Iron Cross. And I am still not sure what my burden is.

The Iron Cross

In the morning, it doesn't take long to pack everything up. After weeks on the road, we all have our routine down pat. Well, almost all. Lloyd has survived the night in his bunk but now starts to faff.

'Have you seen my wallet?'

He turns his rucksack out. No wallet. Heads upstairs to the bar where he last saw it. No wallet. Checks his pockets. No wallet. He's beginning to get worried. He's in a flap and talking fast.

'If I've lost my wallet, I'm scuppered. Everything is in there. All my cards, all my cash.'

Luckily, he is with friends – we can sub him if necessary. While he is emptying his rucksack for the second or third time, each more frantic than the last, I check that my money and cards are not all together.

'Let's completely empty your rucksack. It's probably buried somewhere.'

Pocket by pocket, the pack is emptied again.

'Oh, thank goodness for that – I've found it!'

It was buried in his rucksack after all.

During all of this, Italian Man has been lying on his bed, chewing his unlit cigar. I wonder what he does with it at night? Surely he can't snore with that in his mouth?

We are finally set to leave and head out into the crisp morning. As we climb up through the heather-clad slopes, my mind turns back to the Iron Cross and the burden I will be leaving behind.

Every day since starting to walk, I have held my 'burden' and wondered what it represents. The cool, smooth pebble has revealed nothing. Do I want to release the burden of grief for my mother, who died when she was just a few years older than I am now? This is the day we will reach the cross and I am still not sure.

As we get closer, I am less confident that I will work this out. Everyone else seems to know what they are leaving behind. Why don't I?

Heading up to the cross, I hold my pebble again and turn it over in the palm of my hand. Nothing.

The cross is high in the mountains and the morning is crisp, but the exertion of the climb keeps me warm.

One by one, pilgrims clamber up the mound of stones at the base of the cross and add to it. Having walked with the others for a couple of weeks, I am fairly sure what their burdens are. As they walk up to the cross and drop or carefully place their stones, my heart goes out to them. I lose my composure a little bit more with every burden released.

And then, it is my turn. I follow the path that winds up the mound. As I rise, I realise that I do not want to release the grief I hold for my mother. Instead, I want to carry it with me, not as a burden, but lightly.

It is something else entirely that I assign to my pebble and leave behind with the countless thousands of other burdens.

A Surprise Arrival

As we move away from the Iron Cross, it is light enough to see the landscape in its full glory.

After only five days, my leg is almost completely healed now, so I can look around and enjoy the surroundings, instead of concentrating on every step.

The mountains here are farmed – for timber and power. Far away, a clear blue sky meets a mass of trees on the hills. Wind turbines march along another ridge in the middle distance. On our ridge, the forest gives way to a haze of heather and other herbaceous plants, reminiscent more of Mediterranean landscapes than British moorland.

The temperature does not match the illusion. It is distinctly cool, and I am ravenous, ready for breakfast and a hot cup of tea.

It is not long before we reach a caravan at the side of the path, perched next to a stone cottage. When we order tortilla, the owner heads behind the caravan to cook it in a wood-fired oven.

The caravan and house are both off-grid. The owner and her partner built their home using stone from the abandoned village on the other side of the road. It is the height of summer, and she is walking around wearing a furry hat. I don't blame her. I shiver under my blanket until the warming food and drink arrive, wondering how bleak it must be up here in winter with only wood to use as fuel. They tell us that they are often cut off for weeks at a time. Staying here all year certainly shows dedication to the cause!

After breakfast, we descend from the crisp mountain air back down to warmer, gentler climes. Despite our late breakfast, we stop at the first village for an early lunch. The café's courtyard is full of chattering pilgrims, including a few that we know. Although we are not walking together, they have become an important part of our friendship group. We chat for a while, then head on down through the village.

A man in a blue straw trilby is sitting on a rock at the side of the road, clearly waiting for something. An enormous rucksack rests at his feet. As we approach, he beams and stands up. Lloyd veers over to him and gives him a bear hug.

'Hello, Joe!'

It's a bit of a shock. I have heard about Lloyd's friend Joe. They were supposed to be walking together, but Joe had some trouble with his passport. I had no idea that the issue had been resolved. I had assumed that Lloyd would just be walking with us now.

Even though we have assimilated other people into our family, I immediately worry about Joe and how his appearance will affect our group dynamics and our friendship with Lloyd. I tell myself to keep an open mind and concentrate on my walking, as this section of the path is so uneven.

Lloyd is keeping his eye on me and warns me about every difficult section of the path he comes across. He is conscious that my leg might not be as well healed as I think it is. He waits and helps me where he feels that I might need it. I am reassured. We are not losing Lloyd just because Joe has arrived.

Molinaseca

Somehow, Molinaseca exudes warmth as we approach. It is physically warmer than the mountains we have just crossed, but it is more than that. There is something innately welcoming about the place.

The grey stone church stands sentinel on the upper slopes of the town. We cross an ancient stone bridge over the river where it has been dammed to create a pool. Children are splashing around below us and shrieking in what must still be icy water. A few adults are swimming more serenely, and more are sunbathing on the banks.

Stone buildings line the narrow main street, some with their upper storey plastered and painted. Others have balconies open onto, and sometimes extended over, the street.

The faster walkers in our family have already arrived and are sitting outside a bar in the shade of their umbrellas. There is a Canadian with them who I haven't met before. She is full of smiles, and her name is Marie-Josée – MJ.

It's too early for me to want to start drinking, and I'm avoiding alcohol anyway, so I check into the accommodation we booked a couple of nights ago. A room for four turns out to be separated from the other 'rooms' by a partition wall that does not reach the ceiling. This provides the illusion of soundproofing, without the actual benefits of soundproofing!

The shower is clean but badly designed. The door that opens into the corridor reveals whoever is dressing or undressing. I move as quickly as I can to protect my modesty.

It is always a bonus to find a washing machine in a hostel. This is no exception. Brad and I wait for the machine to become free, wash a load, then hang it on an airer in the sun to dry.

The rest of our Camino family are now rather merry. I can hear them laughing raucously before I even turn into the street they are on. I'm not in the mood for being around drinkers, so decide to explore the town with Brad before joining them for dinner.

This is a small town, with only two streets that run parallel to each other. It does not take long to explore! I am ambling along with Brad when MJ calls us over.

'I've heard the church is open for pilgrims. Shall we go and take a look?'

We agree. MJ is like a ray of light enveloping us as we walk and talk. We are greeted by a tall American man as we approach the church.

'I am on my way home now, but the church will be open for a bit longer.'

The man introduces himself as Tim and tells us that he was also disappointed to find so many churches closed when he walked the Camino. On his return home, he sold up and looked for a church to open on the route. This is it.

I imagine he is a Christian, but his philosophy is that all pilgrims should have the opportunity to sit and reflect as they walk, whether they are religious or not. He opens the church to facilitate this. He asks for our email addresses and sends us some questions to contemplate while walking.

The church is cool and dark, with a collage of flowers on the floor. Peace descends until, with a jolt, I realise it is time to meet the others for dinner.

We walk together back down the hill to a bar on the riverside. Everyone is even merrier now and I am even less inclined to join them, especially as they are showing little interest in eating.

Instead, I sit by the river and call Mike. Every conversation with home draws you away from the reflective pilgrimage experience and back to normal life, so we have talked far less than normal. It's good to catch up.

Over dinner, I realise that leaving my burden behind at the Iron Cross has not worked. It returns with a vengeance. I still have another couple of weeks on the Camino. Perhaps there is time for it to work its magic on me yet. I hope so.

Ponferrada

'Look, it's the castle!'

Brad has been looking forward to seeing the castle at Ponferrada, so we have allowed time in our schedule for a visit. The Camino torturously winds through the town's suburbs to avoid a busy road, but in doing so gives a fabulous distant view of the enormous stone structure.

From here, it is simply imposing. As we near it, it looks even more impressive. The turrets, flags and crenellations of the main entrance give it the appearance of a fairy tale castle, but the rest of the structure tells a different story. Up to three layers of defensive battlements encircle the site. This is a real fortress, not just a fancy frippery.

The castle was built by the Templar Knights, who were charged with protecting pilgrims on the route to Santiago. In days gone past, pilgrims had to contend with threats that we don't need to consider, including bandits targeting them as well as wolves from the forests. I shiver as I think of the hardships they must have endured on their pilgrimages. They would have walked from home, so much further than most pilgrims today. They didn't have technical clothing or GPS to help them find their way. It was more a march of penance than the enjoyable experience it is today.

Instead of having time to ponder this part of Spain's history, Hazel and I spend the morning running around the town, up and down the steep hill. We print out documents from my solicitors, I sign them with Hazel as a witness and then post them. Our Camino mojo has been greatly disturbed by this intrusion from the outside world, and I am glad when we have finished.

It seems that the cool days are over. We are later than usual because of the delay in Ponferrada, so we walk into the heat of the afternoon. After finally fighting our way out of the suburbs, we find ourselves walking through lush green vineyards and forests in the blazing sun. The landscapes here in Spain are big, but because we are walking for so long, we've transitioned through such variety.

I cannot help but smile as I walk, despite feeling rather under the weather. I am back on the trail, doing what I like best, with a group of people who have become friends. I am missing Mike, but hold both emotions at once: sadness at not being with him and the joy of being here. The two sit side-by-side, neither diminishing the other.

No Room at the Inn

We are a few days' walking from the busy part of the Camino now. Pilgrims who walk the final 100km can receive a certificate of completion from the cathedral in Santiago, so the final stretch tends to fill up with people. This is also a holy year, so bumper numbers of pilgrims are arriving in Santiago every day.

After I rise from an afternoon nap, I find Hazel stressed out. The two of us have been booking accommodation for the whole group. We are six now, so it is getting harder, and proving exceptionally difficult for the final stretch into Santiago.

Hazel hands over to me and steps outside for some air. I spend the next couple of hours poring over the guidebook and internet, trying to find places to stay. My Spanish is stretched as I call accommodation providers and am told time and again that they are full. In one town, I call 13 different hostels and hotels, and only manage to secure two beds. I scour the internet with no luck. We are four beds short.

I rejoin the group, frustration painted all over my face. I am getting nowhere and we need to find somewhere to stay. There is always the option of the municipal hostel, but these are filled on a first-come-first-served basis, so there is no guarantee of a bed.

'Let me help.' Joe has noticed my distress. I know that he has authored some books, but didn't realise that he is also a travel agent, with a team he can set to work for us. I give him a huge hug.

'Thank you so much!'

I am glad to have passed the responsibility on to someone else, as I'm sure Hazel is too, and sleep easy in a small dorm with just our Camino family in it.

O'Cebreiro

It's a cool morning up in the hills. We walk along an uninspiring stretch of road until breakfast. I sit outside the café, guarding the bags while the others order food. Ahead, flood meadows flank a lush green river valley. Trees cover the steep banks on each side. A few horses are tethered outside a building a little further up the hill. Today, we are walking up to O'Cebreiro. It is a steep climb and some pilgrims choose to ride to the 9th-century church at the top. We will walk.

A steep slope leads up through the trees. We stop to take a selfie – or rather, to catch our breath. As we are contemplating starting again, Joe and Lloyd stride into view. They are tackling the steep slope as though it was a walk in the park. As usual, they chose to set off later than the rest of the group and catch up with us on the way. Their energy has put me to shame.

I find myself enjoying the exertion of walking uphill, the feeling of achievement at making progress. My cold has disappeared, my leg feels much better, and I am bouncing along, feeling like Snow Light again.

On a narrow path with a steep valley down to the left and heather-clad hills rising to the right, two horses block the way. A groom is with them.

'You can walk behind them. It's perfectly safe.'

We shimmy around their haunches, teetering on the edge of the drop and hoping they are as placid as the groom claims.

We don't have to wonder for long why they are there. They are waiting for a third horse to join them. The groom whistles and in the distance, further up the hill, a white horse raises its head briefly before tucking back into the vegetation lining the path.

For a few minutes, we walk on, keeping half an eye on the white horse and the other half on the view to our left. I can't decide whether I prefer this view of verdant hills or that over the lumps and bumps of ripening wheat on the Meseta. Then I realise that I don't have to decide. It is perfectly possible to love both equally.

Despite the gradient, I am springing up the hill, full of the joys of life. There are shouts ahead; a warning. The white horse is thundering down the path towards us, keen, finally, to join the others and return home. Luckily, there is just room to step to one side as he races past.

As I walk, I ponder the situation with the burden that I theoretically left at the Iron Cross. I confide in Brad to see whether that helps. He listens carefully to what I have to say. His response is immediate and reassuring. One comment is, of course, not enough to make the burden disappear, but it is perhaps a little lighter.

O'Cebreiro is an old stone village with a big, squat church that is open when we arrive. I light a candle in a holder and add it to others forming a waymarker arrow on the floor of the church. This time, I focus on everyone I know and have met on the way who is grieving. I think about my mum and how much joy and love she gave to the world before leaving it far too soon. I appreciate the stillness of the church for a while before rejoining the group and getting on with the serious business of the day – it is time for lunch!

O'Cebreiro appears to be at the top of a hill, but the route magically continues higher into the trees once you leave the village. Although we have spent the day climbing, we are in our stride as we head up and over this final hill for the day.

When we arrive, Joe and Lloyd are already at the hostel, as are our Canadian friends Sara and Karen. Lloyd has been shopping and cooks us a wonderful meal as we relax on our bunks, reading, chatting and dozing. Joe's team has managed to find us accommodation all the way to Santiago now, which has lightened the load, and the mood, especially for Hazel and me. Although this is not the kind of work they usually do, they took our brief and ran with it. All the accommodation they have found is within a stone's throw of the path, within budget and meets our needs perfectly. Now, all we need to do is relax and enjoy the last few days of walking. Dinner is a high-spirited affair that continues long after I have slunk away to sleep.

Hungover

Everyone is jaded after yesterday's exertion and last night's jollity. To our horror, the first part of the route is uphill – again! We are all plodding along, forcing ourselves to continue putting one foot in front of the other. Unusually, we stop in the first village we reach for breakfast, only three kilometres into our walk. Hopefully, this will revive us.

The general malaise hanging over the group this morning is not enough to reduce my enjoyment of the views. We are walking above the clouds that have formed in the lush valleys below us. Despite that, it feels as though we have left the mountains and are now back in the hills. We are making progress towards our goal.

The following morning, as we leave Triacastela, we are surrounded by a gaggle of teenagers in matching hoodies. They exude energy, excitement and chatter on a morning I am feeling weary. We are just over 100km from Santiago now, and I wonder whether this is the way things will be from here, as this is where a lot of people choose to start their journey. Hazel has warned me that the path can get busy from now on. I have vowed to embrace the crowds, but right now, that feels like a step more than I can manage.

I put my head down and drag myself up the hill. It is not long before they are out of sight and earshot ahead. I begin to relax and raise my eyes. The broad path is leading up a wooded valley. As the day brightens, the vibrance of the colours is almost shocking to the senses. Oak trees are sporting light green leaves at the ends of their branches, with those in the shade a far deeper hue. The bluer tints of fir glow right at the top of the valley, where they are catching the sun. Even bluer still, a solitary Blue Atlas cedar stands at the bottom of the valley, in the shade.

Ahead of us, at the edge of the trees, is a small stone building, clinging to the slope. There are no windows on this side and a small wooden cross on the roof. It is not the right shape for a church, and we start to speculate about what it might be.

'Whatever it is, it would make a lovely house. This would be such a wonderful place to step outside with your morning cuppa.' The thought of drinking tea is never far from my mind!

As we near the building, we can see that the door is open and there's a sign outside, welcoming people in. The room is square, filling the entire footprint of the building. An easel dominates the space. Curious, we step inside. The walls are covered with watercolour paintings. One, in particular, draws me in. I gaze deeply into the woods it portrays. There is a solitary walker on the path ahead. 'Walk with me.' The painting speaks to me. I can imagine it on my wall at home, as a daily reminder of the Camino.

It reminds me of 'Footprints in the Sand', a Christian poem I carried with me as a teenager. The writer asks God why he left her in her darkest moments. God replies that there is one set of footprints in the sand at that moment because that was when he carried her.

I no longer believe that God carries you. I believe that it is your friends, family, past experiences and strong foundations that carry you through the darkest times. But the thought of being carried and looked after has stayed with me and helped during the lowest ebbs of my life. All these thoughts swirl through my mind as I gaze into the painting of the lone hiker in the woods, calming me and giving me a sense of deep peace.

The others are chatting with the gallery's owner, Arthur Manton-Lowe. The building was a wreck when he bought it. He renovated it into a small home downstairs and a gallery level with the path. Arthur exudes serenity and Christian love. Each painting includes the quote from John 14:16 'Jesus said I am the way, the truth and the life'. He asks us for permission to say a prayer over us before we leave. Although none of us is Christian, we agree. Who wouldn't want some of that serenity and love bestowed upon them?

A few steps along the path, Hazel pauses, looks at me and says, 'If priests were like him, I'd be a member of the church in a heartbeat.' I nod in agreement. His absolute conviction and life based on sharing Christian love are compelling.

Arthur is one golden thread that makes the tapestry of the Camino so special. There are others, too, contributing in their own way.

Borstal Boys

One of the Borstal Boys is sitting on a wall, his mentor tending to his foot. We have been walking at a similar pace to him and one other for a week or two now, and always exchange a friendly '¡Buen Camino!' as we pass. One of the two has a face that completely lights up when he greets us.

I was curious when I first saw them – a boy carrying a day pack and a man walking alongside with nothing. Brad had read about boys being allowed to walk the Camino with a mentor as an alternative to spending time incarcerated in a borstal – hence our affectionate name for them.

We agree that this seems like a fantastic programme, a chance to have a one-to-one mentor for weeks while walking and learning to manage a budget. The boys have plenty of time to think about where their life is heading now, where they might want to head instead and how to make the transition.

I walk over to check on them, as we do with everyone we see treating blisters or other injuries. There's that smile again, a bit bashful this time. Everything seems under control, so I wish them well and continue my journey.

Donativo

The path is busy with groups of schoolchildren. Vans are parked at strategic places so the pupils can rest, refuel and grab extra supplies if needed. Trestle tables tempt us with piles of snacks and drinks, sadly not for our consumption. Sometimes, we have to pick our way through a throng of students sitting or standing in huddles across the full width of the path.

As with road traffic, groups of pilgrims tend to bunch up on the path, so although it is sometimes busy, there are moments still when we cannot see anyone else in either direction.

As the path wends its way through a jumble of stone buildings, a gate is open into a barn and courtyard. A wooden table is laden with flasks of tea and coffee, piles of bananas and other goodies. A large sign on the table declares that this is a donativo – a place where you make a donation, rather than being charged for the food.

We dive in, ready for a break. A rather dilapidated old stone house stands at the far side of the yard. A wall faces the road we have just walked along, and the other side is open to a smallholding.

Hazel broaches an important issue. 'Do you have any toilets, please?'

The proprietor waves towards the trees. 'If you're having a pee, just go anywhere in the garden, except on the lettuces. If it's more than that, use that compost heap over there.'

The barn has a meditation room and a sign that says 'no wifi, hugging area'. I smile and lurk nearby until I do receive a hug!

Pilgrims are encouraged to paint when they are here. I admire some of the artwork but don't add to it myself. In one corner, scallop shells hang from a branch against the wall. The sign, written in English as well as Spanish, suggests that we think about anything in our lives that isn't serving us well. We are encouraged to leave our scallop shells behind with those negative aspects of our lives and pick another up in Santiago to take forward into the future. I love this idea, and duly remove the shell from my pack and hang it on the branch.

What attitudes are not serving me well? What friendships or relationships don't support me to be the sort of person I want to be? What habits take me in the wrong direction?

Occasionally, an express train of children passes by. Mercifully, they are not enticed by the entrance as we were.

Our break spent in the donativo is longer than usual. We are feeling contemplative, and this is a great space to indulge our need for reflection. Eventually, though, the path calls us to return to our journey.

100km

Hazel has the wind in her sails today. We walk ahead of the group together, passing a few words backwards and forwards, and enjoying the silence in between. We have a target in our sights – the 100km waymarker.

This countryside is astonishing. We are now in Galicia and it feels like home. It is only the details that differentiate the landscape from the UK. The wind turbines rotate on thinner columns. Electricity pylons are a different shape. There are more sweet chestnut trees, and there is a growing number of eucalyptus trees as we head west.

The stone farmhouses and villages are nothing like our own, almost a surprise after being immersed in such a familiar landscape. Each house has a raised grain store, long and thin, on slender stone legs. They are very different from our grain stores that sit squatly on mushroom-shaped plinths. Few of ours remain, yet here, they are ubiquitous, although probably not used to store grain now.

Hazel and I sweep through this countryside, in our stride, and reach the 100km waymarker without a break. The others are in less of a hurry. They have stopped for coffee and we wait for them to catch up.

Their timing is awful. I have just ducked down behind a wall for a pee when I hear laughter. I recognise that voice, it's MJ – they're here, and I've been caught in the act! I stand up and pop my head over the wall. 'Hello!' Laughter erupts; everyone knows why I am there.

We pose for photos at the 100km waymarker. Although it is just a number, the same as any other, it feels significant. We are almost there. Only a few days of walking left to order our thoughts and complete our contemplations.

Thunder

After a hard morning's walk, I am famished. A lot of people stop at this waymarker, yet this is one of the few villages on the path without a café. The vending machine it does have is not enticing, so we continue, hoping we will find something better soon.

A few kilometres further along the route, an elderly lady sits at the arched entrance to a farmhouse and courtyard. As we turn our heads, piles of goodies come into view, stacked up on each side of the covered area. Hot snacks, cold snacks, savoury and sweet.

'¡Hola, buenos días!'

Greedily, I grab a banana, a boiled egg and a croissant, with a cup of tea to wash it down. That should keep me going for a while!

Hydrangeas grow profusely in this area, and this courtyard is no exception. The globes of perfectly formed pastel flowers are framed by matt green leaves. A row of plants, all with blue flowers – and then one that is pink! I walk along the row to an unoccupied table, admiring the profusion of blooms as I pass.

The sky has darkened, and as we finish our food, we exchange glances. 'Is that thunder?'

There is a flurry of activity. The owners are obviously expecting rain. They dash around, putting umbrellas up to keep their customers dry. We take their cue, don waterproofs and cover our packs before continuing towards Portomarín. Our rucksack covers make us look like vivid green beetles plodding down the path.

A little while later, I jump at the sound of a loud crack. 'Has something just been hit?' That was loud. And close. Another flurry of activity, as we all fold and stow our walking poles. The thunderstorm that has been rumbling at a distance is suddenly here. We do not want to walk in an electric storm with lightning conductors in our hands!

As if also cued by the lightning strike, big drops of rain start to fall. Hoods up, heads down, we trudge through the deluge. Water squelches between my toes before bubbling out of the top of my trainers. I wish I had donned my waterproof socks as well as the coat!

It's too late now, my feet are already drenched. It's only another couple of hours until we get to Portomarín, so I continue. I should know better, but decide to take the risk. My feet will be fine.

The path is busy here, with pilgrims congregating in the same place for their overnight stop. Everyone's paths braid like ribbons as we walk at different speeds, overtake and get overtaken by others. There is a rhythm to the walking, each group dancing their own dance, each dance woven into the rich Camino tapestry. There is no jostling for place, just a bright '¡Buen Camino!' like a bead at each weave.

We overtake a woman whose ankle is bent at right angles, such that she cannot put the sole of her foot on the ground. On one side, she leans on a small walking frame. On the other, a nurse supports her elbow. I and my Camino family have had some trials on our journey, but nothing like what this woman is going through. I don't know how far she has walked, but she is still almost 100km from Santiago. I can only imagine that this journey is a true act of faith for her. If I was a Christian, I would pray for her, but as I am not, I send my best wishes into the ether and promise to hold her in my heart until the end of her Camino, just as the nun, Teresa, has done for us.

The rain eases, but that doesn't stop the cold from permeating everything. Cold, wet feet. Cold body. Cold hands. Nothing dangerous, but uncomfortable nevertheless. The rain and the cold seem to dampen everyone's spirits. A queue forms at the top of a treacherous slope between two walls. I am glad of my walking poles as I clamber down, very aware that we will domino down the hill if any of us slips. How is the woman with the bent ankle going to manage this?

At the bottom, we pop out by the river, Portomarín in sight on the other side of the bridge. This old Roman town was once sited low down in the river valley, and the remains of some of the walls can be seen in the river. The town was of such importance that, when the Spanish government dammed the river, the buildings were taken down and rebuilt, stone by stone, above the new water level.

I am ready for a warm shower and dry feet. MJ is struggling, although still smiling. She limps up the Roman steps ahead and our little family splits up as we head to our separate accommodation.

Hazel and I strike lucky. Our hotel has a hot shower and a hairdryer that I use to dry my trail shoes. Our feet have survived walking while wet with no adverse effects. While she sleeps, I head out into the town, refreshed but hungry. A dodgy-looking pizza place does the job. Brad and I eat, joined by MJ when she spots us through the window.

'Oh, good. She made it.' We are relieved to see the woman with the bent ankle making her way along the main street.

After lunch, we find the others in a bar and spend the afternoon laughing and joking together. I am drinking alcohol-free beer, but feel incredibly light-headed when we leave. I can barely walk. Has my drink been spiked? And if so, to what end? I am with a group of friends who would make sure no harm comes to me.

The restaurant we have chosen for dinner is further up the hill. I struggle to drag one foot in front of the other but know that food will help, whatever this is. It seems to take forever to get there, as if I am stuck in a time warp. I sit quietly and eat, hardly aware of the food; just that it is food and food is good. By the end of the meal, I feel tired but no longer spaced out. Our hotel is downhill from here, so I head off on my own, leaving the others to enjoy the evening while I sleep.

By now, the novelty of being with other people every evening is wearing off. These are my friends and I love them all, but I need time away from groups sometimes, to recharge. Every evening, I have to resist the temptation to simply tuck myself in under my duvet (when we have one) and stay there.

Everyone Walks Their Own Camino

A good night's sleep cures so many ills. Whatever it was that ailed me has gone by the morning. The clouds have also gone, my feet are dry, and I relish walking once again, despite the constant hub-bub ahead and behind. We are in a caravan, all heading in the same direction, all with some sort of common purpose. There's something joyous about all these people heading to the same destination.

What is less joyous about this stretch of the Camino is how much toilet paper there is along the path. Perhaps the authorities could provide more toilet stops, or more encouragement to leave no trace.

Many pilgrims are now wearing day packs rather than heavy rucksacks. We are in the zone of tour companies offering hotel accommodation every night, with luggage transported between them. Some of the suitcases with Camino labels on them at the hotel last night were enormous!

My first thought about this is uncharitable. They will get their certificate of completion, and so will we. Yet, we have worked so much harder for ours. I catch myself. That's completely unfair. I have not walked from St-Jean-Pied-de-Port in France – the start of the Camino Francés route. Should I feel like I have somehow walked a lesser Camino? Those who have walked from there did not start from home – should they feel like they have walked a lesser Camino? Absolutely not. I repeat a mantra to myself.

'Everyone walks their own Camino.'

If they take a horse ride up to O'Cebreiro, that's fine. If they taxi some of it (as I have), that's fine. If they only walk the last 100km, that's fine. And for some, like the woman I saw yesterday, that's a far bigger physical challenge than 500km for me. If they walk with day packs and handbags, that's fine, too.

Everyone has different intentions when they set off on a pilgrimage. And everyone has a different journey, even if they start in the same place at the same time. That's the nature and the magic of the Camino. It opens up a myriad of doors, and pilgrims step through the right one for them.

Dog Bite Bongo Drums

The Camino bongo drums are fast at work. Hazel's phone pings. A dog has bitten someone in the next village. The message ripples along the line of pilgrims behind us.

Before reaching any of the buildings, we take the rubber ferrules off the tips of our walking poles so they have a spike on the end. We remove the straps so we can change the grip and use the poles to keep a dog at bay.

We are on red alert as we enter the village, looking around every tree and wall as we approach. Even so, it is not until we have passed the dog – which by now is dozing – that we spot it. We continue quietly, keen to let sleeping dogs lie.

As we leave the village, we put the rubber ferrules back onto our poles. I like to think this is for selfless reasons – the spikes can damage roads and paths in places where they're not needed. But in reality, the incessant tap-tapping of the spike against the hard ground would seriously annoy me if I didn't.

At this point, our family has split up into pairs, walking at different speeds. Joe and Lloyd are behind us. As we re-group in a café, we receive another message.

Joe, who does not use walking poles, has been bitten by the dog.

Smiling Through the Pain

Our feet and bodies in general are all in varying states of repair – or disrepair. Blisters come and go, joints ache and recover, and grazes gradually heal.

My calf is almost completely better. I am in Pepe's debt for setting me off down the path of healing. One of our party is now on serious meds to manage pain from an old injury. Another is limping and grimly determined to stride on.

After the dog bite, Joe is stoic. He is bruised, but luckily, the dog did not break his skin, so there is no concern about infection.

MJ starts to limp so badly we encourage her to sit at the next bench and treat her feet. It is not blisters that are plaguing her, but bruised heels. Every step she takes is agony. Ordinarily, you might stop walking under such conditions, but this is the Camino and we all have a strong motivation to continue.

We break open some ibuprofen gel and I introduce her to the wonders of hikers' wool. This is just wool that I collect from barbed-wire fences or nab from my needle-felting supplies. It's perfect for padding hot spots to prevent blisters. This time, we put a wodge under each heel to provide a bit more loft. I offer to take some of the weight from her bag, but she will not hear of it. Everyone walks their own Camino, and this is clearly a point of pride for her.

We walk on, slowly at first, then faster as the ibuprofen kicks in. I hope this is enough for MJ to be able to continue walking. It would be a terrible shame if she had to stop now, so close to Santiago. She is still laughing despite the pain, so I hope that her positivity will see her through.

Can't Keep Up

Only one day to go. It feels strange, nearing the end of a long hike.

I walk with Brad, significantly behind everyone else. The rest of our Camino family has found their stride, just as we have become used to the slower pace of the last few weeks.

It is as though the others are being drawn to Santiago like steel to a magnet, the draw strengthening as they approach. The same is not happening to me at all. I am keen to continue at the same pace as we have been walking. This is not a race to reach the end, but a process to be savoured.

The seafood in Galicia is excellent. Brad and I dive into a café for lunch. I take my shoes off and cool my feet on the tile floor. Bliss! As we are finishing our delicious sardine sandwiches, MJ joins us. She is concerned about holding us back, but we are in no hurry and enjoy her company while she has lunch too.

MJ has blisters on her feet now, as well as painful heels. She is wincing with every step. Again, I offer to take some of the weight. Again, she refuses. We walk side by side, talking about our Camino experiences, what we have learnt about ourselves and what has changed. As usual, the three of us laugh. A lot.

When she splits off to her accommodation, MJ tells us how much she loves walking with us because our conversation takes her mind off the pain. My heart seems to grow – and glow. What more could you ever want from life than to make things better for other people?

Nearing the end of the day's walk, we call Hazel to find out which accommodation we are both in, assuming that the others are ahead. 'Oh no, we're back in the village you've just passed. We stopped at the café for a long lunch break.'

There's no way we're schlepping back down the hill to meet them. Instead, we find our accommodation. To our mutual delight, the place has a bar and a garden with a large walnut tree providing perfectly cool shade. We chat idly and doze under the dancing leaves until Hazel arrives.

Reaching Santiago

Oh, my goodness! We seem to be on a route march this morning so that we reach Santiago for the lunchtime mass. Maybe the others agreed on this during their long lunch yesterday, but this is not how I wanted to finish my Camino. I struggle to match their pace.

We stop for breakfast, but they are up and out of their seats again before I have finished. I manage to persuade them to stop for a break a couple of hours later. Again, they leave before I have managed to finish and put my pack on.

I am left behind, although thankfully not on my own. Brad is walking at a similar pace, also not eager to spoil the last day by walking as fast as is humanly possible. Nevertheless, we do our best to keep up with the frantic pace of the rest of our group.

The route is less busy and noisy than I feared. It is only once we cross the motorway and into the suburbs of the city that it becomes unpleasant. Traffic is heavy as we pass a series of uninspiring modern sculptures, followed by equally uninspiring parades of shops. The tarmac, pace of the traffic and fumes all jar my senses.

Eventually, we turn into a pedestrian area lined with historic buildings. There are people milling around, but thankfully no traffic or noise.

I know we are close when Hazel links hands with Frank. Brad and I wait for MJ, who is hobbling along a few paces behind us, a look of sheer determination on her face. We three link hands, too.

My heart is thumping hard now. We are almost there!

The sun is rising behind the cathedral spires as we step into the square. We crane our necks to admire the magnificent façade, characterised by round arches stacked above each other. Even the doors are metres above us, reached by a pair of stone staircases forming the shape of a diamond. After so many miles of walking, we have reached our destination. MJ is on her last legs, but beaming broadly. Lloyd and Joe are already there. Every one of us has faced challenges on this journey, but we have all made it. Together.

There is time to register with the Pilgrim Office and receive our certificates before mass, so we continue hurrying until we know that Hazel, Frank and MJ are safely in the service. I am feeling sorely disappointed in the Catholic church, and have no desire to go into the cathedral, however spectacular it is meant to be.

Instead, Brad and I head to a park for some tree shade and Joe and Lloyd head to a bar for some beer. We join them all later for an exquisite lunch, before seeking a garden once again until our apartment is ready.

Lazy conversation leads to lazy eyelids. A gentle smile rests on my lips as I slowly fall into a slumber.

Party!

Brad has had enough and heads for bed after dinner. The rest of us head to a bar and meet up with Sara and Karen. A zero-alcohol beer for me and cocktails for the others fuel dancing, wild laughter and pranks.

MJ is still in significant pain, but she does not let it stop her from having fun and even manages a bit of dancing! She has certainly earnt her trail name of 'Sunshine'.

I sneak off just after midnight into the cool night air. I feel a little vulnerable as I walk through the city on my own. It's a shock being somewhere so busy. Hordes of people are sitting at tables out on the streets, and we are not the only ones partaking in some drunken revelry.

But I am on a mission, so I push my fear to one side. I have heard about a ghost pilgrim at the cathedral and want to see whether the rumours are true. I search the streets. How can I lose something as big as a cathedral? Eventually, I descend a wide flight of steps into a stone-flagged square surrounded by grand buildings. The façade on the right is particularly imposing.

Found it! As I cross the square, hunting for the ghost, a shadow catches my eye. A few more paces and the illusion is complete. The ghost pilgrim is there, hat on head, staff in hand, standing as still as stone. Some say that he is waiting for his lover, others that he is waiting for redemption. Whatever he is waiting for, he provides one final piece of Camino magic to round off my journey.

Becoming Snow Light

On my return to the UK, I was thrown straight back into the hustle and bustle of life. I had an imminent house move to deal with and time away planned with Mike. It was all go.

Of course, pilgrims of old had the whole journey back home in which to reflect on what they have learnt, not just a couple of hours on a crowded aeroplane.

I re-read my diaries in moments carved out of my day. For a while, I wore a shell necklace to remind myself that I was still on a journey. If life was tidy, I would have given myself a clear couple of weeks on my return. But life is not tidy.

As for my burden? The weight of it has lifted. Many writers carry a similar burden - fear that they are not interesting enough or that people will not want to read what they have written.

The biggest lesson I learnt on the Camino is that I must have the confidence to know that I am enough, just as I am. I am not everyone's cup of tea, and that's fine. There are people on the path whose lives I positively impacted. There are people in the wider world whose lives I will positively impact. Others will remain untouched by me, perhaps baffled by me, or even irritated by me. I don't want to cause any negative emotions, but life is too short to be lived muted, in fear of showing people who you are.

I am Snow Light. What a perfect trail name! I want to share my excitement about life, wildlife, landscapes and friendship. And I want to share practical tips and knowledge to help other people feel the same way. Snow Light is a gift I can give to the world. Some will like that gift. Some will not. So be it.

I thought that was it, that the Camino had done its job. Little did I know that it had not finished with me yet!

Section 2:

A Very Different Camino

The Camino Beckons Again

'How do you fancy walking some of the Camino together at Christmas? I'd like to see it for myself and we can use the time to update our ten-year plan.'

Mike and I have had a ten-year plan since we were first married, but so many things have changed recently that it's in a state of disarray. Spending time walking together, enjoying the moment and thinking about the future sounds like a great idea.

'Yes, let's do it.'

Three months later and I'm back in Spain, sprinting through the station towards the last train to Vigo. I can hear Mike's footsteps behind me.

'Please let the doors stay open. Please don't leave yet.'

We could do with some Camino luck right now. Our flight was seriously dclaycd, so we'd missed the last bus. We had trouble finding the train station entrance, and the last train should have left already. Still, I can see it standing at the far end of the platform, its open doors enticing me to run faster.

As I near the train, I force myself to slow to a walk and step carefully into the doorway. A few seconds later, Mike joins me. The doors glide shut behind us as though the driver had been waiting for us. We made it!

As we pass each station, I mentally tick off the places we will be walking through as we head back to Santiago. Padrón, Caldas de Reis, Pontevedra, Redondela. These names mean nothing to me yet; for now, the towns whizz by in the dark, giving us no clues about their nature. We will have to be patient – all will be revealed in time.

Although it's on the Portuguese Camino route, Vigo is in Spain. Unfortunately, we don't have time to walk the whole route from Lisbon or even the shorter and more popular route from Porto. We have just six days' walking ahead. Will that be enough for a 'proper' Camino experience?

I have chilblains on two of my toes. This means I have two swollen and tender toes to fit into my walking boots. The tubes I am wearing to protect them look comical, but they seem to be doing the job. I can walk without too much pain for short distances, at least. I have never hiked all day with such large chilblains. For now, all I can do is hope they won't cause me too much trouble.

We are staying in an apartment close to the route of the Camino. The owners are kind about our late arrival but do not want to interact. We cannot find any food for dinner, the apartment is dirty, and our room faces a street that attracts noisy crowds until the early hours. It is not the best start to our journey.

In the morning, we set off in the dark to visit O Castro, Vigo's castle. Mike collects castles, ticking each one off a list when he has seen it, and over the years, I have come to appreciate them as well. It's a shame I can't say the same about his love of jazz, as no doubt we will visit a jazz club at some point on this journey, too!

The castle stands on a bluff overlooking the estuary but is too far from the port to provide adequate protection. In the past, invaders attacked the town and completely ignored the castle, so it is really little more than a heavily fortified folly. Most of the castle is open to wander through, and the walls largely remain intact. There is far more to see than we had expected. Our journey is already improving!

As the sun appears over the surrounding hills with a gentle orange glow, we get the first glimpse of our surroundings. Evergreen eucalyptus trees cloak the mountains to the east. Below us, Vigo sprawls on the lower-lying land down to a large estuary. The steep-sided Cíes Islands mark the mouth of the estuary, and the open sea stretches to the horizon beyond. The sky is threatening rain. There are just enough breaks in the cloud for a sunrise that promises a bright day. Maybe we'll get lucky with the weather.

Back on the Trail

We collect our bags from our room and check out. Finding our way out of the town is a bit of a struggle. We have not yet tuned in our eyes to spot waymarkers, and the description in our guidebook is not helpful. A local man stops us, points us in the right direction and wishes us a '¡Buen Camino!'

I am keen to get the first stamp on our pilgrim passports as evidence that we have started in Vigo. After a few false starts, we find a café with a stamp and stop for breakfast.

Once we tune our eyes in, we see scallop shells, waymarkers, yellow arrows and images of pilgrims everywhere.

'I really feel like I'm part of something important here. I've never felt that while walking on the UK's long-distance trails.'

Mike is right. Perhaps it's the result of a thousand years of use or the religious significance of the Camino. There is certainly a sense of being a part of something bigger than ourselves.

The well-waymarked path often follows quiet tarmac lanes or trails through woods. Eucalyptus trees shed long shards of copper-coloured bark over the tracks and leave a pungent smell hanging in the air. They are not native to Spain but were planted as fast-growing trees to provide pulp for paper mills. In the decades since, they have become invasive, quickly regenerating where they are not wanted and overshadowing the native oak and chestnut trees. Although it is almost midwinter, the native broadleaf trees show what I think of as autumn hues and have only shed some of their leaves. The same species are already bare at home, resting through the cold, dark months of a British winter.

Mike and I both have a couple of physical niggles, but nothing that will stop us from walking. My chilblains are tender, but the pain is not inhibiting my walking – or my imagination. We talk about everything we would like to do in the future. We know we cannot do it all – there isn't enough time. So, we start to think about what we would most regret **not** doing instead.

Many cafés on the route are closed for winter, so I am glad we are carrying emergency rations. We see a cascade on the map and decide to stop for lunch once we reach it. As we work our way through a bag of nuts and some bread, cyclists pedal past us every few minutes, often calling out a cheery '¡Buenos días!' or '¡Buen Camino!' The waterfalls in the cascade are small and lovely rather than thundering and spectacular – perfect for our reflective mood today.

All day, we walk with the estuary down to our left, watching it narrow as we progress. There are 'hórreos' aplenty here – the grain stores I saw in Galicia in the summer. They are in various states of repair and disrepair – some lovingly maintained, some going to rack and ruin. I smile every time I see one. They are giving me a sense of place, the sense that I am somewhere familiar, even though we are far from home.

On the approach to Redondela, a café has placed advertisements along the path. At the second advert, we exchange glances.

'I hope it's open.'

'Me, too!' We are ready for a break.

As we near the café, welcoming lights glow in the windows above our heads. It's open. The entrance hall is decorated for Christmas, with homemade angels hanging in the windows and a nativity scene complete with a Camino waymarker. We drop our packs and settle into seats by the picture windows. To our right, a large stone church and rows of crosses peeking over a cemetery wall dominate the view. Ahead, swathes of eucalyptus trees drop into a steep valley. Around the corner and out of sight lies Redondela, our destination for today.

Cheered by hot drinks, free cake and a heart-felt '¡Buen Camino!', we step out of the café and circle the church, hoping to find a way in. We rattle every door and try every lock. No luck.

Redondela is a compact town built along a narrow, canalised river. Small wooden bridges cross to a formal park dressed up for Christmas. A viaduct that is also decorated for Christmas runs high over the buildings. Bo Nadal! We weave across the park and through the old streets beyond until we reach a small pedestrian square.

Maria opens the door to the hostel overlooking the square, lets us in, shows us around and makes a recommendation for dinner. She tells us that we are the only guests. The communal kitchen has a kettle – not a given in Spain – so I make some tea while Mike looks around.

'Oh no, I'm so sorry, I didn't realise anyone else was here!' Mike quickly backs into the kitchen. There is someone else here, after all, and he has just walked straight into her dorm.

A few seconds later, Maida joins us in the kitchen, laughing at Mike's error. She is from the Philippines, lives in the US and is five days into her fourth Camino. She plans to arrive in Santiago on the same day as us, although she is taking a slightly different route.

'Why the Camino, rather than one of the many trails in the US?' I ask, curious.

'I'm navigationally challenged, and the Camino routes are well-waymarked. And I feel safer walking the Camino on my own – none of the wildlife here will kill you, and there are more people around.'

We plan to dine together at a restaurant almost next to the hostel. On the way there, we wander through the town. Our first stop is the church, with its circular stained glass window featuring a ring of pilgrim scallop shells and crosses. Then the park by the river, which is resplendent in its Christmas lights.

When we arrive at the restaurant, we are the only people there. It is late for us to be eating – 8 p.m. – but far too early for the average Spaniard. The menu is almost entirely seafood, with no vegetable side dishes or vegetarian alternatives.

We share each dish – octopus, squid and prawns. We dip bread into the serving bowls to soak up the garlicky sauce. I feel guilty for enjoying such delicious seafood. Our oceans are overfished, and almost all sea-dwelling animals are struggling to survive. The least we can do is not make the situation even worse by eating them, yet here I am doing just that.

As we walk back to the hostel, it is cool but dry.

'I'm so glad it didn't rain today,' I remark. 'I hope it holds off for the rest of the week.'

A Good Soaking

My wish has not been granted. It is drizzling as Mike and I head to a café for breakfast. We order tortilla, and when it arrives, we immediately wish we had only ordered one portion. 'Oh well. It will do for lunch, too.'

As we set out from the café, the drizzle turns into rain. We duck under cover to ensure we are fully waterproofed, then put our heads down and start walking. The route is clearly way-marked again, for which I am grateful. I have not been able to download the route onto my phone, so if we lose the waymark-ers, we are walking blind.

Today, Mike and I talk about our values. One of our stron-gest values is to make a positive difference in the world and leave a legacy. Another is to lead an adventurous life. These can some-times conflict, so we muse over how we can achieve both simul-taneously. As we talk, we remind each other of the legacy we have already left in house renovations, our woodland, building proj-ects and people we have helped along the way.

The rain continues through the morning. Sometimes, it pitter-patters on our hoods. At other times, it is heavy enough to drown out the rest of the world. My arms cool as damp seeps through my hitherto waterproof jacket.

At lunchtime, I find that the rain has also permeated our rucksack covers. We have not passed an open café since leaving Redondela, so we perch on the rim of a lavadero to eat leftovers from breakfast. Every village seems to have one of these troughs, usually covered with a roof, that water passes into and flows out of the other end. Angled stone slabs are set around the sides to wash clothes on. Of course, they are not often used for that purpose now, but they provide an attractive focal point and valuable shelter from the rain.

This particular lavadero is not attractive. It is made from concrete, full of silt and overflowing. Two buckets by the entrance are also overflowing – with litter. In most circumstances, we would consider this to be a desolate spot, but having somewhere to sit for a while out of the rain is heavenly.

We bid farewell to the Vigo estuary as we approach Arcade. It is an old Roman town surrounded by hills, at a crossing point of the Verdugo river. As we near the water, we are greeted by swans, crows, ducks and a heron. A series of low, rounded arches span the wide river, supporting the old Roman road. Most traffic rumbles over a new viaduct high over the water, leaving this bridge available for local drivers and pilgrims.

'I do hope the café on the other side is open. I could do with drying off a bit,' I comment as we step onto the bridge.

Camino luck is on our side again. From midway across the bridge, we spot someone leaving the café. We spring over the second half and dive into the dry space. A puddle spreads across the floor from our packs and jackets as we sit with our drinks. My camera has been in a bag under my waterproofs. The bag is sodden, and my camera is wet. Luckily, there is a plentiful supply of paper napkins on the table. To my relief, it is still working. There is a puddle in the pocket I have had my phone in. Another few napkins bite the dust, drying both the pocket and the phone. My pilgrim passport has started to disintegrate, and the ink from the stamps has run; it has gained some character. The pages of my real passport have frilled at the edges; that, too, has gained some character! We apologise profusely to the staff, but they wave our apology away. '¡De nada!' It's nothing. They have seen dripping pilgrims before.

Back on the trail, the eucalyptus trees are particularly pungent, clearing my nose as well as any cold remedy would have done. Their rather peculiar conical nuts litter the paths, some with delicate white flowers still attached.

In a small village, a simple stone chapel dedicated to Santa Marta is open. We have offered to light candles for people as we walk, so we duck in, out of the rain. Sconces hang from the plain stone walls. An aisle leads between two rows of benches to the front, where a high stone table decorated with a laurel branch and two red candles stands on a central support. Three stone shelves protrude from the rear wall, each supporting a statue of a woman – presumably Santa Marta. A pair of white candles flank the central figure. It is a peaceful space in which we sit quietly for a few minutes, dripping onto the stone-flagged floor.

There are no candles to light for others, so that will have to wait. As we step outside, I realise that something has changed. It has stopped raining.

'In the chapel, I asked for the rain to stop,' Mike declares triumphantly. It seems to have worked!

A few minutes later, the rain returns. Laughing, I suggest that Mike might like to be more specific with his requests in the future and ask for the rain to stop for a few days rather than just a few minutes.

Granite is ubiquitous around here. There must be a big quarry nearby, as almost every structure is made from this stone – buildings, walls, posts to hold up grapevines, granaries, the list goes on. In this weather, the stone is a dull, light grey, although I expect it sparkles when the sun shines.

Our guidebook identifies an alternative route into Pontevedra. It sounds idyllic, following a watercourse rather than a road. As we reach the fast-flowing stream, it is still raining. I look to the left, where the path is underwater.

'Thank goodness we're not heading that way!'

We turn right onto a path above the level of the stream. When we find water flowing over the path and into the stream, I am not concerned because Mike's feet are already wet, and my boots are still holding out. I stop to take some photos.

'I'd rather we keep moving, Julia. If the level of the stream rises, we might get into difficulty.'

The stream is close to overtopping, and the valley is wide and flat, so there is no high ground to take refuge on if water levels rise. We push on, cutting corners where possible and following each meander when there is no alternative route. It seems to take forever to reach the town, where the path finally rises to a road.

After a day of walking in persistent rain, we are pleased to arrive at our hostel on the outskirts of Pontevedra. We squelch into the reception area, leaving a water trail behind us. Only two other people are booked in, yet the staff allocate us bunks right next to the man who is planning to leave early in the morning. We rebel and set up in one of the other dorms instead. We can hear the rain pounding down on the single-storey extension as we tumble dry what we can and hang the rest of our wet gear in front of a heater. The room is steaming.

We cannot face the thought of braving the rain again to join Maida for dinner. Instead, we run from our hostel to the nearest restaurant and endure the meal there. It is barely edible, but at least it fills us up. The rain is still falling as we dash back to the hostel.

Lying on my bunk a little later, I think about how grateful I am for having somewhere dry to sleep. The rain is lashing at the window. Will it ever stop, I wonder?

A Silver Lining

We are the only people in the dorm, so we sleep pretty well, even though Mike is too tall to lie straight on the bunk. In the morning, some of our clothes and Mike's boots are still damp. I pad over to the window and open the blinds with trepidation.

'Thank goodness for that. It's stopped raining!'

We have time to explore Pontevedra before we leave. We make a beeline for the purportedly scallop-shaped church, Santuario de Peregrina. It looks unlike any other church we have seen. A tall, highly decorated stone edifice with two squat towers faces onto the square, with a circular building attached behind. Inside, I expect to see scallop-shaped edging, but in reality, it is just a circle with an extension front and rear.

Once I see past my disappointment, I realise that the church is a beautiful, peaceful and special place. The circular nave soars up to a domed ceiling of carved stone. Stained-glass windows and light sconces sport pilgrim scallops. Behind the altar, the decoration is far less ostentatious than usual; a statue of the Pilgrim Virgin, with a few cherubs to keep her company.

I look for candles to light. There are only coin-operated LEDs, which feels like fakery to me. I would prefer to light real candles, although, at this rate, I might not have a choice. For now, I simply sit for a moment with my thoughts.

'Look, Julia. We can go upstairs.' After paying a few Euros, we are allowed to climb to a balcony that encircles the dome above. Negotiating the spiral staircase while wearing a large rucksack is challenging but worthwhile. From the top, you can see the detail of the stonework and feel the true grandeur of the space. Standing on the far side of the balcony with a lamp behind him, Mike is adorned with a halo. Very fitting for a pilgrim!

Mike heads back down, and I catch up with him at the bottom of the stairs. He is talking to a couple of Canadian pilgrims on their way into the church. We are all on the move, so just share a few words before parting. For us, it's time for breakfast. We follow the waymarkers through Pontevedra until a café captures our attention. Cool music drifts from the entrance, and pancakes are on the menu. We're sold! We sing along and even dance a little while waiting for our food to arrive. We are laughing a lot on this trip and enjoying each other's company.

We are on our third day of walking, and our packs feel heavy as we leave the town. Now it has stopped raining, the birds are singing joyfully, helping to lighten our spirits despite our physical tiredness. A deer flicks its white bobtail at us as it bounds gracefully away from our loud human clumsiness.

As the morning progresses, we glimpse the two Canadian pilgrims a short distance ahead. Eventually, we get close enough to call out greetings and bound over to them as they take photos crossing an old bridge.

After stopping to take our own photos, I am surprised that the others have dashed off rather than waiting for a chat.

As we walk through the woods, we talk about possible future work options and our desire to live in an intentional community. We consider the possibility of overseas work, combining our love of adventure with our desire to leave a positive legacy.

Just before noon, we emerge from the trees at the edge of a village. Lights are shining from a café – what perfect timing. The two Canadian pilgrims are relaxing at one table, and a group of Spanish pilgrims are at another. We hover uncertainly. Usually, we would ask to join the Canadians, but they didn't seem to want to talk to us earlier. They solve the problem by inviting us over.

The food is dull, but the conversation sparkles. Mimi lives near Ottawa, where it is minus 40 degrees Celcius at the moment, and her niece Léya lives further west. We learn about why they are walking the Camino and some of the challenges they have faced so far. Mimi started in Lisbon. From there to Porto, the waymarking was sporadic, and the accommodation was widely spaced, so she had to walk long distances each day. She likes to walk in silence, which is why they didn't wait for us earlier. Léya has joined more recently and, like most pilgrims, has been suffering from blisters. We share many interests and agree to meet up for dinner later.

Luckily, we have escaped blisters so far. My toes are a little less swollen now, not causing any trouble during the day, and my hip has settled into the walking routine. On the other hand, Mike's hip is causing him some discomfort. I do not doubt that he will finish the Camino, but I hope it doesn't affect his enjoyment too much.

The good weather continues into the afternoon. Sunlight glints off pools covering every flat area, the land waterlogged or flooded. Rows of vines, devoid of leaves at this time of year, march across the landscape, and birds sing in the trees.

Our guidebook mentions a cascade 500m off the path. We love waterfalls, and after the rain yesterday, we hope it will be impressive today. A map at the end of the drive shows a path up the valley that takes in a series of cascades. We are feeling strong enough for a short detour but are not sure we have either enough daylight or miles left in our legs to see them all. Instead, we decide to admire the falls from the bottom.

We hear the thundering well before we see any water. As we near, a small wooden bridge crosses to an island right in the flow of the river. We look up to see an enormous lump of rock with water cascading over and around it, swirling at the bottom and parting right where we are standing. A cool mist engulfs us, and I laugh with my arms held wide. What power! It was worth trudging through the rain yesterday to see this today.

The bar in the old millhouse feels cosy. A mop and bucket by the door indicate some water infiltration, but a large open hearth holds the dampness at bay. We revive the fire, sit close and enjoy the juxtaposition of safety, comfort and warmth with the thunder of the river just the other side of the wall.

We do not rest for long – it will soon be dark, and we have a way to go yet.

The bridge into Caldas de Reis is busy as we cross it into the town. The vehicle noise and exhaust fumes assault our senses, and it has started to rain again. Initial impressions are not good, but our host is friendly when we arrive at the small hostel, and our double room is warm and comfortable. There's even a kettle and teabags in the kitchen. Things are looking up!

We meet up with Léya and Mimi for dinner. It appears that only one restaurant is open. Luckily, it isn't far as Léya's feet are very sore.

Dinner is a riotous affair. We have made a strong connection with Mimi and Léya, who have immediately become friends. Is this the power of the Camino at work again?

I am beginning to find seafood tapas a little monotonous. Still, the company makes up for the shortcomings of the menu, and the evening flies by.

The imposing church in Caldas de Reis stands in a square lined with dripping palm trees and neatly stacked tables outside dark cafés. It all seems to be biding its time until the sun returns. The church is dedicated to Thomas á Becket, the Archbishop of Canterbury who walked the Camino in the 12th Century, a few years before he was killed. With a connection to the UK, it seems appropriate to light candles here in the morning for our friends.

More Rain

We have developed a routine of walking around each church we come across, trying every door in the hope of gaining entry. It is a disappointment, but not a surprise, to find the Thomas á Becket church firmly locked. Once again, our plans to light candles are scuppered.

The route out of Caldas de Reis takes us through the old town and over a small river. The stone houses feel homely, with Christmas decorations brightening the morning. The Roman bridge is resplendent, bedecked in greenery punctuated with vibrant poinsettia flowers.

It does not take long to leave the town, and as we do, the rain starts to fall. We stop and cover ourselves and our packs in waterproofs that we already know will not keep us dry. At least it's mild, so being wet is merely uncomfortable and not life-threatening.

I wonder whether it was worth the effort when we are overtaken by a local out with his dog, with just an umbrella to keep him dry. The rain intensifies into a steady downpour shortly after he has passed, thundering onto our hoods and shutting out all other sounds. We see him chatting with another dog walker a mile or so later, and I am glad we dressed for the rain. He is drenched from his chest down, with his trousers plastered to his legs, although his dog is trotting around as though he is acclimatised to this weather. Our waterproofs are at least keeping some of the rain at bay.

The valley is sometimes wooded, with native trees fighting for space with the pungent and fast-growing eucalypts. At other times, it opens out into grassy fields. We emerge onto a fast road, where we have to wait for a couple of minutes to be able to cross safely. Surely there'll be a café here we can stop at to shelter from the rain? No chance. Instead, we dive into a bus shelter and perch on the bench inside.

My mind turns to thoughts of comfort. 'I don't know about you, but I could do with a proper sit down in a café.'

'Yep, I agree.'

We set off again into the rain, hopeful but not optimistic that our wish will come true.

'Look, Mike, they say the Camino provides, and it has. It's a café, and it's open!' I almost skip down the path and in through the door.

Three local men are chatting with the man behind the counter. It is not quite midday, and one is already supping a glass of wine.

I peel off my jacket and reveal my wet shoulders. Mike is also soaked. We will need to return our expensive jackets when we get home, but I don't dwell on the thought. I am intent on drying out and ordering refreshments.

As we finish our food, the man with a glass of wine catches Mike's attention and shows him some pendants he has made. They are cleverly designed, and I am pleased that Mike buys one. Or rather, two – one cut out from the other. I like the idea of wearing these matching medallions when we are apart.

Eventually, and reluctantly, I force myself back into my wet jacket and out into the ongoing downpour. There's no chance of suffering from dehydration today!

We spend the afternoon discussing our future and how we can best leave a legacy, which we have always considered particularly important.

'Whatever we do, I'd like to keep it simple,' muses Mike. 'One thing I will take from this walk is how much better things are when you keep them simple. My previous plans were far too complex.'

At the edge of some woods, we spot a stone building with a plaque. It's an old watermill standing close to a small stream. Mike admires the quality of construction and how the builders have carved a single length of stone to carry water into the mill. The leat is no longer in use, so the mill is dry. The only light in the small room is from the open door and one tiny window. Once our eyes adjust to the dark, we see that the workings have gone, but the big, heavy stone mill wheels remain. I do not envy the miller – this would have been a cramped, noisy and deeply unpleasant environment to work in.

The rain stops briefly on the final leg of today's journey into Padrón, a town famous for its Russian roulette peppers. Most of them are sweet, but occasionally they are fiery. I ate a lot of them in the summer, none of which were hot – and then bought a batch in the UK that almost all were. Unfortunately, we won't be able to eat any on this trip, as they are not in season.

We are almost dry as we approach the hostel in the industrial suburbs of the town, and then it starts to rain. Again. We dive under the door canopy and try to gain entry. The door is locked, and we can see there's no one at the reception desk. A notice on the door says to try a café nearby. When we arrive, the server initially looks baffled. Ultimately, though, she manages to find a code for the door and the numbers of our bunks.

'Hello, Julia! Hello, Mike!' Léya and Mimi are already in the hostel, relaxing in their bunks.

Mike takes on laundry duties, washing and drying our clothes, while I relax for a couple of hours. Léya is in even more pain but soldiering on. She has Santiago in her sights, and nothing will stop her from getting there. I give her some of my foot care kit to use in the morning, hoping it will help.

Léya, Mimi and Mike all have lukewarm showers. I do not want to make myself cold, so I decide I can live without this evening.

'Lukewarm showers are a part of Camino life that I won't miss!' Mimi declares. This is the first lukewarm shower I have heard about on the Camino, but she has rarely encountered a hot one.

We all head out for dinner to a place that has been recommended to us, close to the hostel. The rain has eased, so the walk is not too much of a trial.

The restaurant reminds me of an alpine sports bar, with pine cladding decorated with framed sports scarves. A television showing a football match fills one wall.

I like to try new things, and I'm bored with the usual seafood offering. When I see pigs' ears on the menu, I want to give them a go.

'Julia, I asked the server about the pigs' ears. You know they're boiled, don't you?' Mimi is not sure about my choice.

Léya agrees. 'Won't it just be like eating layers of cartilage?'

'Let's try them and see. We've got plenty of other food if we don't like them. We've been eating the same food for days, so it'll be good to try something different.'

I imagine they will be simmered in a flavoursome sauce, slow-cooked like the pigs' cheeks I so enjoyed during my summer Camino. I could not have been more wrong. A massive plate of strips of plain-boiled ear turns up. Mimi was right. So was Léya. The texture is like alternate layers of cartilage and fat. Mike chews a piece, blanches and gags. The others try it, pull faces and spit it out. I manage slightly more before admitting defeat and moving the plate to one side, out of sight.

'Perhaps they would have been better deep fried,' offers Mimi. However they are cooked, it will take some doing to coax me to try them again.

The rest of the meal – and the evening – are thoroughly enjoyable. We learn more about life in Canada, tapping maple trees, collecting honey from hives, and the cave Mimi and her husband plan to use to age their homemade cheeses. We offer to help with any or all of those activities, and Mimi accepts. I hope she is serious!

Léya and Mimi are both Métis – being people of mixed European and Indigenous ancestry, and one of the three recognized Aboriginal peoples in Canada. Léya has been learning about Métis culture and tells us about their history. Some voyageurs – mainly French men who traded in furs and transported them across Canada by canoe in spring, summer, and fall, then by dog-pulled sleds during the winter – married Indigenous women. Over time, their mixed-ancestry families created their own communities and their unique culture emerged. As with many other ethnic and Indigenous groups, they have suffered from persecution and racism. Now there is some sort of financial compensation available, disagreements sometimes occur over who is genuinely part of the community, which can be divisive. I reflect on colonialism, delusions of superiority and fantasies about purity of bloodlines – and what an almighty mess these concepts have created worldwide.

Back in the dorm, my mind returns to more prosaic matters. I hang our damp belongings around the bunk area to dry out overnight. Mike has a trapped nerve that is making him fidget. The bed creaks every time he moves, so he decamps onto a sofa in the lounge to avoid disturbing the whole dorm during the night.

The dorm only has half a dozen occupants and is quiet and dark. I set my alarm for 8 a.m., sure everyone else will be up and moving by then.

A Stealthy Exit

I sleep well, wake a few minutes before the alarm and turn it off. The dorm remains quiet and dark. I sneak out to use the bathroom and check on Mike in the lounge. He is awake and packing up. I will have to sneak back into the dorm and pack my things up as quietly as possible in the dark, so I don't disturb the others.

I load everything I can into my sleeping bag and carry it to the lounge to pack away. My rucksack is in a coin-operated locker, and there's no way to open it without a loud clunk. Sorry, guys! I involuntarily step backwards as stale, musty air gushes from the opened locker and assaults my nose. Leaving my damp pack in an enclosed space overnight was not a very clever idea!

Padrón is believed to be where St James started his ministry in Spain. The original stone from which the town takes its name stands under the altar in the church. Some think this stone is the mooring post for St James' boat, others that it was a Roman altar dedicated to Neptune. Either way, we would like to see this important artefact, so after breakfast, we go to the church.

It is mid-morning, so we expect to find the church open. Once again, our hopes are dashed. Fancy leaving such an important church locked!

We still haven't yet found a church in which to light candles. It's hard to believe that so many churches are inaccessible on a major pilgrimage route.

Another couple of friends have asked us to send blessings to them from somewhere beautiful and somewhere special. I start to worry that we have already passed the most beautiful spots – the Vigo estuary and the cascades – and that we will not be able to fulfil their request. Although this countryside is pretty, I would not call it beautiful, and it is becoming less attractive the closer we are to Santiago.

We are both a bit weary today. Mike's lack of sleep and the lack of fruit and vegetables in our diet are taking their toll. The rain is not helping, either.

We walk through numerous villages where every house has at least one citrus tree in the garden.

'Wouldn't it be lovely to eat some of this fruit?' I comment as we pass a laden orange tree. It seems like such a shame to walk past when so many of the fruits are falling to the ground. Like apple trees in the UK, each orange tree must produce far more than a family can consume.

A few minutes later, we notice a man standing at his garden gate, with an orange in each hand, waiting for someone.

'Look, isn't that nice - he's picked some oranges for his friend.'

Mike agrees.

As we near the man, he starts to look in our direction. Nearer still, and his face breaks into a smile. He speaks to us in the fastest Spanish I have heard yet. I don't manage to pick up a single word, but his intention is clear. He has seen us coming and would like to give us a gift. He holds a melon-sized orange out to Mike and a slightly smaller one to me.

'¡Muchas gracias, Señor! You are very kind.'

What an incredible gift, and just after talking about our desire to eat some fruit. We now have the most enormous oranges we have ever seen in hand and equally as big smiles across our faces. The Camino has provided again.

After walking through forests and quiet backwaters, it is a shock when the path starts to follow a fast, busy road. The noise, the speed of passing vehicles and being covered in spray are all profoundly unpleasant. Luckily, the path turns away after a few hundred metres.

At 11:30, we agree to stop in the next open café for lunch. It could be just around the corner or miles away. We shall see.

Half an hour later, we find ourselves at a crossroads in a quiet town with an open bar. We dive in and once again peel off our wet outer layers to sit in our damp inner layers. Still desperate for some vitamins, we order vegetable pizzas and orange juice – the best of a limited choice.

The bar has three televisions, and as we wait for our lunch to arrive, we are both mesmerised. The weirdest show is being broadcast. It's a lottery draw, but not as we know it! As balls spew from two separate lottery machines, two children dressed in what appears to be school uniform chant and pass the balls to an adult adjudicator. This continues for the entire hour that we are waiting and eating. After a while, the children and adjudicator are replaced. They continue to chant the same lines repeatedly, along with the numbers on the balls. The droning chants are occasionally interspersed by film clips of the winners holding up cheques and popping bottles of fizz. We have stumbled on the annual Christmas lottery, which continues all day. Every time we pass a television in a shop window, bar or home, the same scene is being played out with a different set of people in the frame.

I am pleased to leave the chanting behind, even though it means heading back into the rain. It is not long before we are walking through woodland again. Leaves crunch underfoot, and the trees occasionally shower us with heavy splats when the breeze shakes their rain-drenched branches. I fill my lungs with fresh, tree-filtered air and find another smile tickling my lips. At the edge of the trees, a flock of goldfinches lifts my spirits even further. How could they not, with their excitable chatter, flashes of gold as they fly and striking red faces?

We continue to discuss our plans and start fleshing out some timescales for change. We want to keep life as simple as possible while contributing to society, leaving a legacy and being adventurous – not always a straightforward combination! We tend to complicate life by filling our diaries, trying to do too much and achieve too many aims with each activity. We want the simplicity we have experienced while walking the Camino to percolate through our lives, giving us space to think, enjoy what we are doing and just be.

In a small village, we stop to admire the lavadero. Initially, I assumed the lavaderos were covered to protect those washing clothes from the sun. Having walked in Galicia for a few days now, I realise it might also be to protect them from the rain. Our friends who requested a blessing showed us similar washing areas by the rivers in France. Every time we see one, we are reminded of our friends, so we realise this would be a perfect place to send out a blessing.

I stand by the running water, bend down and scoop up a handful.

'May the rain water your crops in summer when they need it,

Just as this water flows to the sea.

May the sun shine on your faces,

And a gentle wind blow at your backs.'

We continue to circle every church we pass, trying every door to gain entry. I wish I knew how to pick locks! I am beginning to wonder whether we will ever be able to light candles as we promised.

Locked Out

Milladoiro is not far from Santiago and looks and feels like a new satellite town. Our hostel occupies part of the ground floor of a modern apartment block, with a shop and café on one side. Although we arrive during the advertised check-in time, the door is locked, and the room beyond is dark. There's a phone number on the door. I ring it and leave a message on the answerphone. The phone number on the booking website has an automated message that tells me to ring the other number. I leave another message – we will wait in the café next door.

Despite drinking tea and eating some hot food, my core temperature slowly drops as we sit in wet clothes, waiting. I add layers to keep warm, but it doesn't work. I am damp and tired and need to dry off and warm up. Another call, another message left. I ask the people running the café whether they know the hostel owners. Apparently, it's the church, but that doesn't open until two hours after the café closes. The café staff ring the number for the hostel and receive the same automated response.

'Lo siento, no puedo hacer nada más para ayudarte.' There's nothing else they can do to help.

Just before the café closes, Mike heads back to the hostel to see whether it's open. It is. The staff are friendly and welcoming and light a fire in the hearth – an unexpected bonus on a cool and damp winter's day. We pay to use the clothes dryer and get a code for the door, so we can get back in when we go out for dinner.

Knowing that we have access to a dryer, I wash some clothes. Mike puts everything through the dryer in batches. The first batch almost dries. After that, everything comes out steaming rather than dry. The staff have left, and there's no easy fix we can find. Once again, we hang all our damp things up around the dorm in the hope it will be a little drier by morning.

I sit next to the fire to warm myself up and resist heading back outside into the rain for dinner. We hunt around to see whether anyone has left any food in the cupboards, but they haven't. We're going to have to go out. Armed with the door code, we let the door close behind us.

'Oh no!' We should have tested the code with one of us still inside. Rookie error! We try the pin pad and find that it is dead.

There's nothing we can do now, so we send a message to the owners and head to the town centre to eat. We find a cosy bar with good food and some vegetables, although not many. By the time we finish, we have not heard back from the hostel.

'Perhaps they've fixed the door and haven't bothered to tell us,' I say, hopefully. No such luck. The pin pad remains dead, and there are no messages from the owners. Four other people are staying in the hostel, and we can see a couple of them sitting by the fire. We can't reach the window we are looking through – there are metal shutters and an outdoor seating area between them and us.

We start discussing our options for attracting someone's attention when one of the pilgrims we met earlier walks past the door. We knock furiously. At first, her expression is not friendly. We continue to bang on the door and wave until she realises who we are. Thank goodness we spoke to her earlier – we're in!

We chat for a while with a Korean pilgrim, taking this opportunity to learn more about the region's geopolitics. She, in turn, films us for her YouTube channel. She and the others head to bed one by one, leaving just the two of us sitting by the fire. We add a log and chat for a while before deciding it is time for us to follow. As we still have lots of damp clothes, I hang them in front of the fire, hoping this will help them to dry overnight.

Reaching Santiago a Second Time

Most hostels we have stayed in on this route have automated timing on the dorm lights. This has sometimes left us groping around in the dark to set up and pack away our sleeping areas. This morning, the opposite happens. At 7 a.m., the light at our end of the dorm comes on. I wake immediately and look towards Mike, who is also now awake. We might as well get up.

I head straight to the lounge to retrieve our clothes from in front of the fire. Thankfully, they are almost dry.

We step out in the dim light of dawn into a day that never seems to brighten fully, but at least the rain holds off for a while. Not long into the walk, we glimpse the cathedral across the far side of a valley, where three dark spires pierce the horizon.

'I didn't realise it's built from grey stone,' says Mike.

'It's not – it's golden. Just not in this light!'

The first part of the walk into the city is delightful, along a wooded valley and through small villages – although all the churches are, as usual, locked. As we approach Santiago, we come across two waymarkers pointing in opposite directions. We refer to the guidebook and find that one route is longer through quiet suburbs, and the other is shorter along a busier road. Neither looks very attractive, so we choose the shorter one.

We pass through vibrant communities and quickly arrive in the heart of Santiago. We skirt a park I recognise from the summer and dive into the labyrinth of old streets around the cathedral. I last walked these streets in blazing sunshine. This time, dark clouds hang overhead, and big, well-spaced raindrops start to fall. We pick up our pace. As we approach the cathedral, the rain begins in earnest. We shelter under the arches of the City Hall to admire the cathedral's magnificent facade. We have made it!

In the summer, I was so disappointed in the Catholic church that I didn't want to enter the cathedral. I am going to this time, but there are things to do first.

The Cathedral Office is quiet. We are the only pilgrims there. It takes moments to print our compostelas – certificates of completion – and head back out of the building. The next stop is our hotel, which is somewhat more downmarket than we would like at the end of a long trek. We drop our bags off and return to the cathedral. According to our guidebook, there is a route that pilgrims have been taking through the cathedral since time immemorial. We try to follow the same route. The compass directions in the guidebook are muddled and do not match those on the ground. We finally get our bearings and find that the Jesse tree and the statue of St James, both vital elements of the tour, are cordoned off. Security guards patrol the cordon. This part of the cathedral is only accessible to people who buy a ticket from the other side of the square. Once again, the Catholic church has put barriers in the way of pilgrims.

So, instead of following the route through the cathedral taken by countless pilgrims before, we walk the length of the church towards the monstrous, glinting gold and silver statuary above the choir. It is similar to that of Burgos Cathedral but even bigger and more ostentatious. Here, St James is not 'just' whipping a Moor as he is at Burgos. Instead, he's slaying him with a sword. The iconography and messages here are even stronger than those that made me so angry at Burgos.

I turn away, take a deep breath and concentrate on feelings of love and concern for others. I have finally found some candles to light for those I have made promises to and want to be in the right frame of mind. I spend a moment thinking about each person. I fill my heart with peace and love before I light each candle, sending my blessings into the universe as the flames flicker into life.

We admire the cathedral's architecture for a few more minutes, then descend a few steps to view St James' shrine. We are both a little baffled about why human remains are venerated in this way.

When we are ready to leave, we find the exit is through the gift shop. We pretend to browse, not wanting to brave the rain slamming against the glass doors.

Eventually, we make a dash for it across to an arcade in front of a hotel and bar. We dive into the bar and order hot drinks. The bar itself is a bit of a dive, so we don't stay long. The rain has eased a little as we hurry back to our hotel, although it is still bouncing off the pavements and running in rills down the streets. We want to explore Santiago, but sightseeing is never much fun when it's cold and wet. Instead, we hole up in our hotel room and listen to the rain pounding down on the street below.

'I wonder whether there's any jazz in Santiago this evening,' Mike muses. An internet search reveals a few possibilities, but nothing certain, so a couple of hours later, we venture out into the rain to see what we can find.

We also have some practical things to attend to – we need to print our boarding passes for the flight home and find out about buses on Christmas Day. The Pilgrim House is a centre in the heart of the city that welcomes pilgrims and offers practical and spiritual support. We receive a warm welcome, the help we need, and an invitation to their party tomorrow, on Christmas Eve.

Mike is concerned that it will be an evening of staid prayer, and I think there will be music and dancing. Well, I hope so, anyway. We can always leave if it's not for us.

We zigzag across the city, hunting down the bars that might have live music tonight. Some of them don't seem to exist. In the others, the bar tenders shrug.

'Not tonight, sorry.'

On the verge of giving up, we come across a deliciously fragrant packaging-free shop with a young man behind the counter.

'I'll just go and ask him.' I think this is a strange choice, but there's no harm in standing in the shop, sheltering from the rain and feasting my senses on the piles of herbs and spices. The young man frowns, seemingly working through the city in his head.

'Let me check.' He turns to his computer and searches for a bar. 'They sometimes have music, but it isn't clear whether they do tonight. It isn't far – you could go and ask them.' He gives us directions, and we are there just a few minutes later. There will be music, but they are not serving food. The bartender recommends a restaurant nearby.

We arrange to meet Mimi, Léya and Maida at the restaurant, as they all arrived in Santiago today too. More seafood, more wine, more great company. After dinner, we leave the restaurant for the bar and music. When we arrive, the shutters are closed and locked. I run round to the other entrance, which is also locked. We wave and knock, but the man inside – the same man we spoke to earlier – ignores us. How utterly disappointing.

We find another bar, without music, for a quick drink. We don't stay up late because we have a big day planned for tomorrow.

Closure

Loud revellers pass below our hotel window all night, keeping us awake. We barely have a wink of sleep.

Maida has hired a car for a day trip to Finisterre and Muxía, both traditional endpoints of the Camino on the Atlantic Ocean. Many pilgrims walk for an additional four days to reach the 0,000km waymarkers at one or other of the two places, and sometimes both.

I am grateful for being whisked along in a car, comfortable and dry. The old bridge at Brandomil, the most westerly town of the Roman Empire, has water swirling around it. The Romans would have had to paddle to reach it on a day like today. Luckily, the more modern road bridge is above the level of the floods, and we are safe to continue to Finisterre – the end of the world.

We walk beyond the lighthouse onto the rocky headland. It is wild, the sea crashing onto rocks below. We lean into the wind and whoop with joy.

We stand side by side, thinking of our friends who requested a blessing from somewhere beautiful. They would love this spot, with views across the ocean, dramatic cliffs vanishing into the distance and seabirds wheeling above and below. We quietly wish them well.

I have been here once before – at the end of my summer Camino, but today, something new happens. Today, I feel a strong sense of closure. After a month of walking in the summer, several months of reflection and another week's walking, I have finished my Camino. I have done what needed to be done. I have a clearer idea of who I am, and Mike and I have built the foundations of our new 10-year plan.

We both feel this is a more fitting place to finish our Camino than the cathedral in Santiago. Being somewhere elemental appeals to us far more than being in a city, as we love to feel the power of nature and our own insignificance. Cathedrals are, I suspect, designed to give you a similar experience – to feel insignificant in comparison to the power of God.

The rain holds off for our trip along the beautiful coastline to the south, then north to Muxía in time for sunset. As we drive, there is a glimmer of promise that the clouds will part for long enough to see the sun set, but that glimmer winks shut after a few moments.

Muxía is very different to Finisterre. Here, you can get right down to the sea. You can stand on the shore and feel the spray on your cheeks. You can hear the waves pounding on the rocks and taste the salty air. Here, you feel the power of the waves more than the wind. This is an incredible spot, so we send more blessings on the wind to our friends. This time, we include all our friends and family struggling with any aspect of their lives.

With our Camino complete, there's just a party and Christmas Day Mass before our journey home and the start of the next phase of our lives.

The Energy of Love

Neither of us was right about the party at Pilgrim House. The room is busy and buzzing with energy. The smell of Christmas tempts me towards a cauldron of steaming mulled wine. More temptation calls from the buffet table; slices of meats and cheeses, bowls of hummus with crackers, succulent cherry tomatoes and bunches of grapes. A man sits with a guitar on his knee, occasionally picking it up and strumming a few notes.

There is no dancing, but there is plenty of conversation. I sink into a sofa with a plate of food and introduce myself to the woman sitting nearby. She is radiant and relaxed. After some small talk, she tells me about her Camino experience. She was brought up as a Catholic but had fallen out with the church and God when she was drawn to walk the Camino. One Camino led to another until she had walked five in two years.

'During this period, I saw so many people helping others that I started to feel there is something greater than us working through us. Because of my Catholic upbringing, I trust that this love-energy is God. I allow it to guide me, and it has brought me back to the church. To me, God is not some supernatural being judging us, but the energy of love.'

She now works on the Camino, providing support to pilgrims. She wants love to shine through her and attract people to find that energy for themselves, whether or not that's through the church. Some of her radiance has transferred itself, and I am glowing as we head back to our hotel. The idea of the energy of love flowing through us all, joining us together as one, is appealing. The concept fits perfectly with that of Snow Light, the trail name I was given and adopted during my summer Camino.

I think back to that Camino and Pepe, the healer. Perhaps it was the energy of love working through his hands that healed my leg. I think back to the friendships I formed with my Camino family and the way we all supported each other in our personal quests. I think back to Teresa, the nun who promised to hold us in her heart as we walked. Throughout my life, people have been generous to me: my family, gymnastics coaches, Girlguiding leaders, strangers who gave me a bed for the night when I was walking England's South West Coast Path, and countless others. Perhaps the energy of love is the unifying force that has supported me through all the trials of life. Perhaps it is the energy of love that leaves only one set of footprints in the sand.

Christmas Day Mass

No one is sure when the Christmas Day Mass will start, but they do seem confident that the Botafumeiro, a giant incense censer, will be swung. We sit in the church with Mimi, Léya and Maida, waiting patiently. The three of us who were not raised in the Catholic tradition feel like fish out of water and sit together so we can make a quick getaway if we want to.

Eventually, a security guard in a high-viz vest announces the start of the service. Not the most promising way to introduce the proceedings!

A group of robed men process into the nave, and the service starts. The pageantry does not appeal to me, so I hope the Botafumeiro will be swung; that is why we are here. Several men group around a rope hanging from a pulley way up high in the transept. The rumours must be true – they are preparing to swing it! My heart skips a beat. I have heard this is spectacular, and I hope it is worth the wait.

Another man fills the large silver censer with hot charcoal, and then the Botafumeiro starts to swing. Each pull of the rope lifts it higher, incense billowing out. The censer arcs towards the roof space of the church until it almost reaches the horizontal. It is moving so fast that I can barely keep track of it. My heart is racing. This is indeed a spectacular sight.

Suddenly, it's over, the swings shorten, and the Botafumeiro slows to a halt.

The spectacle of the Botafumeiro is followed by a droning, monotone sermon. I am glad we have a flight to catch and an excellent excuse to leave.

It is time to say goodbye to Santiago and the Camino. For now, at least.

Section 3:

Your Camino

Walking Your Own Camino

You have heard about my journey on the Camino. Now, it's time to start planning yours.

I feel that I should start by addressing the question of religion. The Camino is a spider's web of routes across Europe that meet at Santiago de Compostela, where St James the Apostle's bones are enshrined in the cathedral. Pilgrims have walked the Camino for the last thousand years.

These days, hundreds of thousands of pilgrims walk the Camino each year, but for most, religion is not the driving force. For my Camino friends, our reasons for walking varied. We walked to achieve a physical and mental challenge, process grief, and re-discover our place in the world. We walked for the sheer joy of putting one step in front of another and for the peace and mental clarity you gain on the trail. And we walked to spend time with friends and family, whether they were by our side or in our thoughts. Only a few had any connection to the church or walked for religious reasons. The Camino is open to everyone.

In **Live Your Bucket List**, I detail a process to follow to make your bucket list dreams come true. If you dream of walking the Camino, one important part of the process is to learn from others – there is no need to reinvent the wheel.

The following chapters allow you to learn from my journey to make yours the best possible success. Each chapter contains things to consider when planning your Camino and to help you reflect on your return. The Appendices provide information on accommodation, places to eat, packing lists and choosing your Camino and some ideas for prompts to turn your Camino into a pilgrimage.

You can download a free planning sheet from: www.juliags.com/camino.

If you prefer writing in a notebook, all the questions and considerations below have space for your answers in the **Walking the Camino Supplementary Workbook**, which is also available from www.juliags.com/camino.

Walking the Camino is likely to throw up some challenges. If you are passionate about your journey, it will be far easier to continue, so the first stage of the process is to ignite your passion for your plans.

Ignite Your Dream

Walking the Camino is hard work. It takes effort. Most of us are not used to walking day after day, with weight on our backs. You will need to be fit and prepared for discomfort and setbacks.

The process described in **Live Your Bucket List** will help you overcome obstacles to achieving your dreams. I have summarised some key points relevant to walking the Camino here. You can listen to the full Ignite Your Dream milestone of Live Your Bucket List, free of charge, at <u>www.juliags.com/liveyourbucketlist</u>.

The first step is to decide precisely what you are planning:

- How far do you want to walk? Or for how long?
- How far do you want to walk each day? We found that 20-25km a day worked well, and we walked at around 4km an hour. On the days we walked further, the last few kilometres felt like a slog. Some prefer to walk faster and further each day. On some Caminos, you might need to walk further each day to reach the next available accommodation.

- What time of year do you want to walk? The summer can be intensely hot, and unless you are an experienced mountaineer, it would be best to avoid crossing the Pyrenees in wintry conditions. Many pilgrims choose to walk in spring or autumn to avoid these extremes.

- Which route do you want to take? The Camino Francés is the most popular, but many other options exist. See Appendix 1, Choosing Your Camino, for help in deciding. Sara Dhooma, who has walked multiple Caminos and is one of my Camino friends, has written this appendix. Check out her YouTube channel for lots of hiking and Camino inspiration.

- Will you carry your luggage or use a transfer service? On the Francés route, the hostels had information from luggage transfer companies detailing how to book your bag with them. In 2022, the cost was €5 per bag. You do not need to book in advance, but check that this service is available if you want to use it.

- What type of accommodation would you prefer? See Appendix 2, Accommodation, for information about the choices available.

- Are you going to walk alone, with a friend or in a group? All these options are popular – whichever you choose, there will be others doing the same thing.

- Will you organise everything yourself or join an organised tour?

Once you have defined your dream in more detail, you may find it helpful to consider how to overcome any potential stumbling blocks.

- What are your reasons for not having walked the Camino already? These might include a lack of fitness, not having someone to walk with, needing to save up, or struggling to find the time.
- Are there any other reasons you can think of why you might shy away from the challenge now? What limiting beliefs do you have that might stop you, e.g. I'm too old, too young, not good enough, can't afford it? What do you fear if you pursue this dream?

For each of these potential stumbling blocks, what can you do to smash or sidestep it?

The final step to fully ignite your dream is understanding your 'why'.

- Consider all your reasons for wanting to walk the Camino and the strength of each.
- Then, consider all your reasons for NOT wanting to walk it and the strength of each.
- Do the positives outweigh the negatives? If not, is there anything you can do to strengthen the positives or reduce the significance of the negatives?

That's the logical element of decision-making covered. It would help to make a decision that sticks if you are also emotionally engaged.

- How will you feel once you have achieved your dream? Picture yourself standing outside Santiago cathedral.

Who or what will you be grateful for? What skills have you developed? What challenges will you have overcome?

- And how will you feel if you don't pursue your Camino dream? Imagine how you will feel in a year, five years and ten years. How does this compare to being committed to achieving your goal?

If you're not bothered, this exercise should help you realise that, and you can focus on a different dream instead.

Conversely, if you are now excited and want to do this, then it's time to agree on dates with your walking companions and start planning your trip.

Make a Plan

If you break any challenge down into chunks, I find that it makes planning easier.

- What resources do you need? Check out my packing list in Appendix 4. Is there anything you need but don't have?
  - Do you have a comfortable backpack?
  - What will you wear on your feet? In summer, trail shoes are likely the most comfortable option, and you might want to wear warmer, waterproof shoes or boots in winter. Do your existing shoes or boots have enough wear left in them for the distance you will walk?
- What training do you need to do? How long do you think you will need to get fit enough? Building up to a 16 km (10 mile) walk with a full rucksack two days in a row worked well for the distances we were walking. If you don't have time to train as much as you would like, then look for somewhere to start where you can walk for

shorter days while your fitness builds. The first couple of days' walk from St-Jean-Pied-de-Port, the start of the Camino Francés, is almost all uphill as the route crosses the Pyrenees. It can be particularly punishing for those who are not fit.

- How about logistics?
  - How are you going to get to the starting point?
  - Do you want to book accommodation for the first couple of days?
  - Do you need to book time off work or other commitments?
- How can you make time to reflect and recover on your return? Many pilgrims walk or take a bus to Muxía or Finisterre and spend a few days there after reaching Santiago. I recommend not diving back into the busyness of life when you return home but taking time to reflect and make any changes you want to.
- If you want to turn your Camino into a pilgrimage rather than just a long-distance walk, how will you do that? Do you have questions you would like to ponder? Are there people you want to think about and light candles for? See Appendix 5 for some suggested prompts.

One key element of planning is learning from others who have completed the same or similar challenges. I learnt a lot from my friend Hazel who had walked the Camino before. You are already taking a step towards this by learning from my experience.

- Who do you know who could help you prepare for the Camino, either spiritually or practically?

- What books could you read? I recommend Carolyn Gillespie's account of her Camino experience in **Pilgrim: Finding a New Way on the Camino de Santiago**. You will almost certainly benefit from reading a guidebook, too. These tend to break the routes down into stages, giving distances and elevations and providing information about accommodation and sights along the way.

- What YouTube videos could you watch? I have enjoyed watching Sara Dhooma and Homemade Wanderlust for information and inspiration about the Camino and long-distance hiking in general.

- Which podcasts could you listen to?

- What Facebook groups or other forums could you join? Many pilgrims find the Camino de Santiago Forum a useful resource.

Here are some recommendations from me, a seasoned walker but a novice pilgrim. As with any advice, take what you find helpful and ignore anything that won't work for you.

- Guidebooks do not necessarily contain detailed maps, as most routes are well-waymarked. On the Francés route, I occasionally used the Buen Camino app to check we were heading in the right direction.

- Keep your pack light. How much you carry is likely to impact your enjoyment, and a heavier pack is more likely to lead to blisters and injury. See Appendix 4 for my packing lists.

- Buy a 'credencial' - a pilgrim passport - before you leave. If you are in the UK, you can get these from the Confraternity of St James. Although you can pick these up on the trail, having one when you set off saves you from hunting for one on your first day. If you collect stamps in your pilgrim passport as you walk, the Pilgrim Office of Santiago Cathedral will issue you a certificate on arrival in Santiago.

- Learn a bit of Spanish. Not everyone speaks English, and nor should they have to. I find it also feels good to try to communicate with someone in the local language.

- Walk at a pace that suits you. I'm more likely to injure myself when I walk faster than is natural for me.

- Consider your dietary needs. You will use more calories and need more vitamins and minerals than usual. I take iron tablets when walking long distances because, in the past, I have suffered from anaemia on long treks. Generally speaking, I found the mix of food good on the Francés route, but I suspect I would have benefitted from some multivitamin tablets on the Portugues route.

- If you are walking the Francés route, carry a stone representing a burden. Think about it as you walk, and leave it behind at the Iron Cross.

It can be helpful to think about what might go wrong on your trip and prepare for it as far as is sensible.

- What's your preferred method of dealing with blisters? Do you have a blister treatment kit on your kit list?

- Do you have any physical weaknesses or injuries you need to consider, e.g. a knee that might need strapping?

- Do you know basic first aid? Would you like to be able to help fellow pilgrims if they get into trouble? Professional medical support is unlikely to be far away, but early intervention helps. On both Caminos, my first aid kit focussed on things that might go wrong when walking – a blister kit, a dressing for grazes and a bandage for twisted ankles. What will you include in yours?

- Do you know the signs of dehydration or heat stroke? What can you do to avoid these conditions? During the summer, we started early so we didn't have to walk through the hottest part of the day. I drank half a litre of water before setting off and refilled my bottle at every opportunity – on the Francés route, every village had a drinking fountain. I carried 2.5 litres of water and never got close to finishing it. We didn't see anywhere near as many drinking fountains on the Portugues route.

- Do you have travel insurance? Primary medical care is available in towns and cities, and of course, there are hospitals in the cities. You might need to pay for treatment, though.

- What would you do if someone stole your pack or other valuables? We reduced the risk by always leaving someone outside cafes with the bags. I recommend carrying your most valuable items with you and splitting your cards and money into different bags and pockets. I wish I had had a dry bag for my valuables when I was showering – there isn't always a lot of space to keep things dry. Petty theft rates in Spain are high, so it's worth being vigilant.

- Conversely, the crime rate in Spain is low overall. You are unlikely to be attacked by a person while on the Camino, but do you know what to do if you are? The emergency number for Europe is 112. On the Francés route, I also saw posters giving a number for the local police.

- How will you protect yourself from any unfriendly dogs you encounter?

- Are you taking any essential medication? If so, I recommend always carrying it with you and splitting it between two locations, as you would with money.

- What will you do if you need to pee or poo and are nowhere near a toilet? I carry a pee cloth for the former and for the latter, a few dog-poo bags and some toilet paper. Luckily, I never had to use the poo bags.

- What other contingency situations do you foresee?

As part of your planning, take a moment to think about your strengths and how they could help you or other pilgrims. They might have nothing to do with hiking, but they can still be helpful. For example, if you are calm when things don't go to plan, you will be an asset to any group. If you can sing, you could stop at intervals and lift pilgrims' spirits with a song.

Also, consider your weaknesses. How can you sidestep, manage or overcome them?

The final two elements of your plan are to consider how you will find the time and the money to complete your dream.

- When can you fit in training? Is there something else that you need to stop doing for a while to give yourself more time?

- Do you need to book time off work for the trip itself? If you can't take enough time off to walk the entire route, could you walk it in sections instead?

- How will you carve out some time to reflect on your experience on your return?

- How much money do you need? In 2022, I spent around €40-50 a day staying in mid-range hostels and eating well. If you need to reduce cost, could you borrow any kit you need? Would you be happy to forego coffee in cafes and drink water at the side of the path instead? Is there a pilgrimage closer to home you could do that reduces transport costs? Could you walk a shorter distance to keep costs down?

- How long will you need to save up, or can you pay for it from your savings or income?

Once all these elements are in place, it's time to get out there and implement your plan.

Implement Your Plan

Planning is an essential part of the process, but a plan means nothing until you put it into practice. It's time to get moving!

If you're lucky, everything will go smoothly, but when has that ever happened in real life?

When things get bumpy, you can help yourself stay on track using some simple techniques.

One is the power of self-talk:

- What mantras could you adopt to help you when things get tough? Try saying them out loud to yourself to give them more power. My confidence ebbs and flows, and the simple 'You've got this' often gives me the boost I need.

- What negative stories do you tell yourself that might get in the way, e.g. 'I'm too old to walk long distances'? What can you do to change these stories? There's no need to lie to yourself. Just think about how you can reframe things. For example, would the thought, 'If I train well and pace myself, I will succeed,' serve you better?

When completing a challenge like training for and walking a long distance, looking after yourself is more important than ever.

- What must you do to look after your health while training and walking the route?
- Do you need to eat particularly healthily or take supplements?
- Do you need to ask someone to be more positive or supportive? Do you need to avoid someone while you are completing this challenge to protect your positive state of mind?
- If you are an introvert, how will you ensure you have enough time to recharge between social interactions? The Francés route in the summer is busy, but I found enough quiet time in the afternoons to sit alone on my bunk and recharge.

Sometimes, an unforeseen event will threaten to knock you off course. If that happens, try reviewing your reason for walking the Camino. Then consider your options:

- Do you need to shift your attention to deal with this unforeseen event and park your pilgrimage dream for now?
- Can you adapt your plans, e.g. tackling a shorter route closer to home?
- Are there any new advantages to gain from this unforeseen event?
- Can you still do something towards your Camino dream? If not, is it time to consider tackling another bucket list dream while you can't pursue this one?

If you want to make the most of your experience, read on for one final stage of the process.

Reaching Santiago - Celebrate and Reflect

Congratulations on completing your pilgrimage! How do you feel - excited? Satisfied? A bit deflated? At the end of any significant challenge, it is natural to feel a sense of disappointment that it has ended, as well as excitement that you have achieved your goal.

Some of my Camino family framed their certificates of completion, pilgrim passports and souvenirs they picked up on the way. Up on the wall in their homes, they will provide a regular reminder of their achievement.

- How are you going to mark your achievement?

Writing this book and giving talks about my Camino experience has helped me consolidate my memories of the two Caminos I walked.

- How will you consolidate your memories?

This is also an excellent time to reflect on your journey. One of my greatest lessons from the summer Camino was that not everyone will like my writing. I'd love it if they did, but I must accept that some people will not – and that's OK. The winter Camino reminded me that walking can give you clarity of thought and help you and your walking companion to work through issues together. My husband Mike and I now have a vibrant plan for our future, which I look forward to sharing with you in due course.

- What have you learnt about yourself on your Camino?
- What have you learnt about others?
- How have you changed?
- How will you apply this learning to your everyday life?

Appendices

Appendix 1 - Choosing Your Camino

I met Sara Dhooma while I was walking my summer Camino. Sara has hiked many of the Caminos across Spain and from further afield. Here, she shares her thoughts on how to choose your Camino:

A pilgrimage to Santiago de Compostela can start from just about anywhere. I have followed many official European Camino routes over the past ten years. Choosing the best route for you depends on the season, how fit you are and why you are walking the Camino.

Time of Year

You can walk the Camino de Santiago in Europe at any time of year. For most routes, the peak season is spring to autumn, when the walking conditions are delightful, and the weather is often gorgeous. Pilgrims flock to the popular routes from around the world, so you'll meet all sorts of people. Unfortunately, the popularity of the Camino at this time of year can mean that there is a race to reach the budget hostels, as many do not accept reservations. Pilgrims sometimes queue up before the hostels open, hoping to find a space. When hostels are full, showers can become lukewarm, the kitchens crowded, and the dorms noisy.

If you walk in winter to avoid the crowds, you will need to take warmer sleeping gear, making your backpack heavier. You will also need waterproofs to protect you from the cooling Galician rain. You may need to complete long walking stages, take your tent, use taxis or stay in hotels, as many pilgrim lodgings close in winter. The mountain routes can become treacherous in wintry weather – always check the trail conditions with locals before heading out. Having said all that, a winter Camino is fantastic for reflection and quiet walking.

Your Fitness Level

You need not be super fit to enjoy walking the Camino de Santiago. You can start with short daily stages if you are a novice long-distance walker. I recommend walking less than 15km for the first few days in these circumstances. If you keep your itinerary flexible, you can choose stage lengths that fit with how your body is responding to the challenge. I have noticed that some pilgrims set a schedule and then push through injuries to meet it. This can result in significant damage and prematurely end their Camino journey.

It is good practice to build extra days into your schedule so you can rest if your feet or knees hurt or you have some other physical malady. If you have limited time, consider walking one section of the Camino or choose a short route to finish in Santiago de Compostela.

During peak season on the busy routes, you can arrange to have your luggage transferred to your next accommodation for a small fee. This can alleviate the stress of carrying a heavy pack. It is challenging to walk a long distance up and down hills, and the freedom of a small daypack can make your journey far more comfortable. Luggage transfer is also useful for pilgrims carrying heavy kit, such as photography gear or a CPAP machine.

If you train before your trip, you are more likely to enjoy your pilgrimage. The Camino routes often have hard flat surfaces, which can be more stressful on your body than a soft and more uneven hiking path. Learning how to manage blisters and other walking injuries during a training period at home is easier than on the Camino. Training can make the difference between being exhausted in the evening and having enough energy to explore.

If you are walking fit, you can also choose between more routes. The less popular routes can have long daily stages – sometimes as far as 40 or more kilometres – and cross remote, mountainous areas with tricky trail conditions and limited services.

Why Do You Want to Walk the Camino de Santiago?

Knowing the answer to this question will help you to choose your route. Every way has its own charm. For example, if you are interested in Roman history, you will love the ancient path and historical sites of the Via de la Plata. I have made some suggestions about route selection below. Beware! If you complete one Camino, you will probably want to try others.

If You Are an Inexperienced Walker

The two most popular routes, the Camino Francés (764 km) and Camino Portugues (620 km), offer a gentle introduction to long-distance pilgrimage. The terrain is varied, and navigation is simple, with frequent waymarkers. There are plenty of amenities such as hotels, hostels, cafes and shops, so there is no pressure to hike long stages. There is a wealth of incredible cities, ancient churches and tiny villages to explore. Walkers are also well supported with things like luggage transfer services and public transport links.

If You Love Nature

The coastal Camino del Norte (824 km) and the mountainous Camino Primitivo (313 km) both offer delightful walking through verdant hills, plenty of wildlife and astounding views. Both are strenuous with significant elevation changes. Trail conditions can be dangerous in poor weather, and you must be prepared to deal with rain, mud and maybe snow.

If You Are Short of Time

The two shortest Caminos are the Camino Inglés (119 km) and the Camino San Salvador (130 km). On the Camino Inglés, you walk along the coast for two days before heading inland through the Galician countryside to finish in Santiago.

The Camino San Salvador is physically demanding and ends in Oviedo rather than Santiago. This short but marvellous route through the mountains offers some of the prettiest landscapes in Spain.

Alternatively, start in Sarria on the Camino Francés or Tui/Vigo on the Camino Portugues to walk the last 100 km into Santiago – enough to earn a Compostela certificate from the Pilgrim Office.

If You Love Food

For foodies, the Via Pondensis from Puy-en-Velay (1500 km) and the Via Lemovicensis from Vezelay (1747 km) extend across different French regions. Both routes allow you to delight in the local gastronomy, including meat simmered in rich sauces, wonderful cheese and exquisite truffle dishes. Pilgrims often stay in gîtes that provide dinner, bed and breakfast for a set price. These meals are usually fresh and delicious, with generous proportions – just what hungry hikers need – and are often finished with an entire cheese course. You can pick up gorgeous pastries in village bakeries for a mid-afternoon boost. The higher costs of food on the French Caminos are undoubtedly worth it.

Within Spain, the Via de la Plata (970 km) is a great foodie choice. The Extremadura acorn-fed Iberian ham has a distinctly nutty flavour and is divine.

If You Love Solitude

Finding solitude on the more popular routes during peak season is difficult. Instead, try them in the colder, wetter months.

Less busy routes include the Camino Mozarabe (619 km from Almeria) and the Ruta de Lana (676 km). It is best to be walking fit for these historical pilgrimages, as the distance between places to stay can be long. The path may be lonely, but locals still give pilgrims a warm welcome. I highly recommend these routes for Camino veterans looking for a unique Camino experience.

For more Camino and other hiking inspiration, check out Sara's YouTube channel: www.youtube.com/saradhooma

There are some official Camino routes in the UK. However, they don't tend to have the same quality of infrastructure as the Spanish routes. The Confraternity of St James is a good organisation for information about these routes: https://www.csj.org.uk/caminos-in-the-uk

Appendix 2 - Accommodation

There are few camping options, and wild camping is illegal in Spain. However, there are hostels in most villages and hotels in some. We used the Buen Camino app to find accommodation on the Camino Francés. We found booking.com helpful, and guidebooks also tend to list most of what's available.

The cheapest place to stay is usually the municipal hostel, and most operate on a first-come, first-served basis. In the summer, we preferred to book a couple of days in advance so we knew we had somewhere to stay. As we approached Santiago, there was a lot of pressure on accommodation, so we had to book further ahead. In the winter, Mike and I booked all our accommodation in advance, as so few hostels were open.

In the hostels, the dorms are of variable size. The largest we stayed in had 40 beds in one room, and the smallest had just two. Many have bunk beds. The best bunk beds are sturdy, surrounded by partitions on three sides and a curtain on the fourth, high enough to sit up in and have a socket to charge your phone. Many do not meet this standard!

Most have plastic covers on the mattresses, and you are often given thin disposable sheets to place over the top. It's a good idea to check any seams in the mattresses for bed bugs before you use them and to take a sheet sleeping bag as a minimum to sleep in. A lightweight blanket is also a good idea. There is a lot of hype about bed bugs on the Camino. However, we didn't see any sign of them, possibly because of the new cleaning regimes introduced due to the COVID pandemic.

Dorms are usually mixed, and many pilgrims sleep in their underwear. Most people did not flaunt their semi-nudity, and I did not notice anyone taking an inappropriate interest in other partially-dressed pilgrims.

Some pilgrims are, of course, more considerate than others. Please take care not to shine your head torch in anyone's face. It is a myth that a red lamp will not disturb people – any bright light shone on your face will wake you up. Most of the time, there is enough ambient light in the hostels not to need a head torch. If you are moving around when others are asleep, be as quiet as possible and be quick. If you tend to snore, please do what you can to minimise the disturbance to others, for example, lie on your side.

The facilities in hostels differ. If having a washing machine or kitchen is important to you, check before you book. All hostels have showers, although, as Sara and Mimi both said, they can be lukewarm. Most have somewhere you can hand-wash clothes and airers you can hang them on to dry.

While walking, I heard rumours that some hostels had blocked or locked fire exits. I don't know whether they were true, but it's always a good idea to check your exit routes in case of a fire.

However safe a hostel feels, most are not secure. Some have lockers or drawers with locks, but in most, you have to trust that no one will walk off with your belongings. To this end, I recommend always keeping your valuables on your person. Unless you are travelling with a friend, use a dry bag to take them into the shower with you, too. While sleeping, my valuables were inside my sleeping bag with me rather than loose to one side. I didn't hear about any thefts, but if you are not careful, it would be easy for an opportunist to steal something.

Appendix 3 - Places to Eat

Along busier Caminos, there are plenty of places to eat. Most villages have a small shop for supplies, and the towns and cities have the usual choice.

In busy places, many hostels and restaurants offer a pilgrims' menu in the evening. Pilgrims' menus are typically three courses with wine or water and usually provide good food at an excellent price.

During our winter Camino, many cafés and restaurants were closed, and we didn't find any pilgrims' menus. There was little choice in most places we stayed, and sometimes only one restaurant was available for evening meals.

Cafés often had tortillas and croissants for breakfast, and lunch was typically a cheese and ham baguette.

Our guidebook pinpointed mobile food van spots, but you can't guarantee they will be there when you are. Having that additional opportunity for a break and some sustenance was always a bonus! Another bonus was the people who set up stalls at the side of the path, some of which were donativos – places where you make a donation rather than paying a fixed price.

On both the routes I walked, it would be difficult for vegetarians and vegans to find good food, but I understand it is not impossible. You might want to take a supplement with you in case you end up eating a restricted diet.

Appendix 4 – Packing List

I like to keep the weight of my pack down as far as possible while remaining comfortable. Here is the list of what I chose to take with me. Add or subtract anything you like – this is just a guide!

Summer Clothes

- Sunhat
- Underwear – 2 bras, 2 pairs of knickers, 2 pairs of socks with loopy soles, 1 pair of inner socks, 1 pair of waterproof socks
- Leggings – 2 long, 1 short
- Tops – 1 loose long-sleeved shirt, 1 short-sleeved technical top, 1 long-sleeved technical top, 1 lightweight fleece
- Waterproofs – 1 lightweight jacket
- Footwear – 1 pair of trail shoes, 1 pair of lightweight trekking sandals
- Silk shawl
- Drybags for everything

Winter Clothes

- Beany hat
- Underwear – 2 bras, 2 pairs of knickers, 2 pairs of socks with loopy soles
- Leggings – 2 long
- Tops – 2 long-sleeved thermal tops, 2 lightweight fleeces
- Waterproofs – 1 lightweight jacket, waterproof trousers
- Footwear – 1 pair of waterproof hiking boots and 1 pair of lightweight trainers
- Silk shawl
- Drybags for everything

Other – Summer & Winter

- Travel blanket
- Super-lightweight travel towel
- Small section of carry mat to sit on (used more in winter than summer)
- Kula pee cloth, toilet roll and dog poo bags
- Head torch
- Adapter for European sockets
- Battery pack
- Phone, earbuds
- Camera & tripod
- Phone and camera charging leads
- Spare memory card and battery for camera
- Spare specs

- Glasses case to use at night
- 2 clothes pegs & safety pins to hang damp clothes from my pack
- Tenacious Tape – fixes almost anything!
- Earplugs – silicone worked better for me than the foam ones
- Iron supplements and multivitamins
- Tissues
- First aid kit – hikers wool, toe gel tubes, blister care, bandage, gauze, tweezers to remove ticks (not used), nail file, painkillers, anti-inflammatory tablets, antihistamines, etc
- Guidebook – I found the paperback version easier to use than the ebook
- Notebook, propelling pencil
- Passport, GHIC card
- Pilgrim passport (credencial)
- Cash
- Lightweight carabiner to hang things from my rucksack
- Backpack
- Washbag – nail scissors, insect repellent, deodorant, soap/shower gel, toothbrush, suncream (summer), face cream, small tube of toothpaste, sewing kit

Other - Summer

- Sheet sleeping bag – silk
- Lightweight water bottle, 2-litre hydration bladder

- Walking poles
- Ribbon to tie walking poles together at accommodation
- Fan

Other – Winter

- Sleeping bag
- Lightweight water bottle, 2-litre hydration bladder, flask for hot drinks

I wish I had also taken

- A lightweight walking umbrella to attach to my rucksack. An umbrella will help keep you cool in summer and dry in winter.
- A lightweight day pack that doubles up as a dry bag.
- Possibly a penknife (beware of confiscation at the airport!)

For more detail about the kit I took on the summer Camino, check out my YouTube channel:

https://www.youtube.com/@JuliaGSAuthorSpeaker

Appendix 5 - Pilgrimage Prompts

If you want to turn a walk into a pilgrimage, here are some prompts that you might find helpful.

- What burden do I carry that I would like to leave behind? How can I do that?
- What are my values? How can I live my life by these values?
- Who do I know who bolsters my mood and confidence? Can I spend more time with them?
- Who do I know who damages my mood and confidence? How can I protect myself from them?
- What attitudes, beliefs or habits serve me well?
- What attitudes, beliefs or habits no longer serve me? What could I replace them with?
- As I near the end of my life, what will I most regret having done or not done? How can I limit those regrets?
- What difference would I like to make in the world? How can I make that happen?

- What legacy have I already left?
- What do I like about myself?
- What do I like most about the people I love?
- What do I like about my life?
- What do I most dislike about my life, and what can I do about that?
- What am I grateful for today?
- What am I grateful for in my life at home?
- Who would I like to hold in my heart and my thoughts as I walk? How am I going to do that?
- Who would I like to light a candle for?

Bonus Section:

A Different Perspective

Having written so much about my 'Camino family', I thought you might like to hear a little about their experiences on the Camino.

Joe Cameron

This was not my first Camino, nor will it be my last. As always, I loved the walking, the food and the scenery. Lloyd and I met through work and hit it off, but we live on different continents. Walking the Camino allows us to spend time together and build our friendship. We like to walk fast and play hard. We always meet lovely people, and I always go home with terrific memories.

Of course, I didn't enjoy being bitten by the dog, but I have fully recovered, and it won't put me off walking more Caminos in the future.

I know some people walk the Camino for spiritual or religious reasons, but that's not the case for me. Lloyd and I choose the Camino because the routes are easy to follow rather than because it's a pilgrimage. Even with all the waymarkers, we manage to go the wrong way sometimes – imagine what it would be like trying to follow a path that was not well signposted! On the Camino, we can just concentrate on making friends and enjoying the scenery, food and company without the stress of following a map.

When I walk at home, I find myself stopping to look at maps a lot, which reduces the enjoyment of the trip and interrupts the rhythm of walking. I recently did a short walk that was so badly waymarked that my GPS tracker tells me I spent over an hour map reading. When I'm on holiday, I would prefer to make things easy and not have to concentrate too hard.

Hazel Eyton-Jones

So, here I was. About to walk my second Camino. Why was I doing it? For me, that was easy to answer... it was more like, 'Why had I left it 7 years since my first one before doing another?'

So much had changed since my first Camino. I was older, I'd survived breast cancer, my fitness levels weren't as good as they were the first time, and we'd had 2 years of lockdown with Covid-19. But I couldn't wait to be walking to Santiago de Compostela again. Finally, with a spring in my feet and a smile on my face, I was back in Saint-Jean-Pied-de-Port and ready for 'the off'!

The first time I walked it, I went on my own. Friends and family back home had thought I was mad! Why would I walk more than 800km across northern Spain alone? Would I be safe? What would happen to me? How would I cope on my own? Would I get lost?

Although nervous, I was confident all would be fine. So many people walk the Camino each year that I wouldn't be alone unless I chose to be. Spain has everything I could possibly need should I find myself without something or needing assistance...

and I spoke enough Spanish (just!) to get by. I met so many wonderful people from all over the world and made a bond so strong with my fellow pilgrims that despite the miles separating us, we remain firm friends to this day.

A few years after my first Camino, my Australian friend said he'd like to walk it but felt unsure about going on his own. I offered to be his walking buddy, and so the planning began. We planned and planned, booked tickets and got excited. Then cancer forced me to rethink and delay. A year later, we started the planning again, and I began to work my way back to health and improve my fitness. Having done the Camino once, I was under no illusion as to how tough the walking could be. Those first couple of days up and over the Pyrenees are brutal if you're out of condition!

Tickets were booked again, and we set our sights on leaving in spring 2020, but Covid-19 had other plans. We rescheduled. Then we rescheduled again. Finally, on 31st May 2022, we flew to France.

After so much planning and forced changes, I couldn't quite believe we were back!

People walk the Camino for so many different reasons. It's been a pilgrimage route for hundreds of years. In more recent times, people do it for other reasons too, be it spiritual, a personal challenge, a way of disconnecting from everyday life, to reset and reconnect with themselves and/or nature, to really experience walking through a country or to be a part of something bigger than themselves. People say, 'you walk your own Camino,' and that applies to the 'why', 'with whom', and the 'how'.

What was it that brought me back?

Certainly, it's a challenging walk. It's not necessarily the distance or the elevation. You can always manage those things by doing shorter days, taking breaks or starting earlier. It's the fact that you're walking every day, day after day. But there are ways to manage that. Walk shorter distances for a day or so, or take a rest day. That's the beauty of the Camino... you walk what works for you, not some prescribed daily distance.

For me, more than anything, it's the chance to reconnect with what is simple in life, to enjoy the here and now. Life really is very simple on the Camino. You wake, pack your rucksack, walk, eat, find somewhere to sleep, wash yourself, wash your clothes, eat, sleep, and then repeat. Everything you need is on your back. It's very liberating to realise that all the stuff you have at home is just that – 'stuff'. As the days go by, there is time to reflect, time to meet new people, time to see new things, time to notice the world around you, and time to just be. There is time. Something we have precious little of in today's world.

It's also one of the very few times in life when people you meet genuinely want you to succeed and reach your goal. I haven't met anyone on the Camino who wanted to succeed personally at the expense of another. Quite the opposite. It's second nature to help your fellow pilgrims in whatever way you can. They say 'the Camino provides'... and it really does. If you need your faith in human nature restored... go on a Camino. You won't be disappointed.

Mike Goodfellow-Smith

Simply Put – One Step at a Time

I had a plan for my sixties: buy some land; self-build or renovate some houses; grow food; and bring together hordes of like-minded people into an intentional community. It needed my full commitment, physically and financially. And it was complicated, with lots of moving parts.

A few months ago, my wife, Julia, started quietly saying she wasn't as enthusiastic about my plan as she once was. Of course, I was sure Julia would snap out of this negative nudge in due course, and we always agreed that if I was insistent, we would do this grand project. But of course, Julia had quietly sown the seed of question about my grandiose plan.

Whilst this was percolating, I had a busy schedule as a full-time lecturer for one university and a part-time lecturer for two others. I provide training for the European Union Climate KIC programme, and we have a consultancy business, Quest for

Future Solutions. There was also an interesting list of maintenance jobs and potential projects at our new home, membership of Llanelli Rotary and trusteeship of another local charity. So life was already quite complicated, exciting and fulfilling – and sometimes, challenging.

So how to sort out / balance / realign our complicated lifestyle of full engagement in trying to make a positive contribution to society? It had to be a walk. At university, I often send students off to 'walk and talk'. Walking and talking really does help clarify what we think, feel and plan. So a walk it had to be, and up stepped Julia with her cunningly conceived... I mean, perfectly timed plan.

'Let's walk the Camino together.'

The plan was to walk from Porto in Portugal to Santiago de Compostela – about 215km. However, I just could not fit the time in for that length of walk. So, Vigo to Santiago de Compostela was the agreed route – just 90km, 5 days of easy walking. In this instance, I had nothing to plan – Julia booked everything and planned the route. This was a first – normally, I do all of this, but Julia is now a walker, writer and public speaker, and could take on this role much more readily. So this was super easy for me. I could concentrate on deciding whether I wanted to continue with a complicated lifestyle, make it even more complicated with substantial risk, or take an alternative route.

Now, I could give you perspectives on the walk that may well be different from Julia's, but for me, the most important feature was the simplicity of walking the Camino. On my back was a 10kg pack. The essentials for the next few days were all there, bar food and water. We had a simple room or dorm bed booked every night. All we had to do was walk, unpack, eat, sleep and repeat. And that is just what we did, along with meeting some beautiful new friends and seeing spectacular views, the awesome natural power of stormy waterfalls and the birds and bees that Galicia put in our path.

The simplicity of knowing the path, putting one foot in front of the other and getting your posture and kit aligned gives your body and mind a chance to react. Steady walking at a steady pace allows one's mind to cut those Gordian knots we tangle in our lives. It helped me see alternatives not yet considered, not contemplated and not examined.

For some, it is right for them to continue with grand plans. For me, the simplicity of walking the Camino has thrown into perspective a new way of making a positive difference in society without having to rely on financial support and loans, without worrying about many moving parts, and without dependence on so many different people.

For me, this simple path to Santiago has now become a simple path to contributing to society. To boldly go to countries not visited, not lived in, and not properly experienced. To volunteer on projects that people need help with. To make some of the trips that I have rejected in the past, succumbing to carbon guilt. But wherever possible, we will get to places with the least negative environmental impact possible, contribute to environmental and social projects whilst there and leave a positive legacy. I will see the world I have dreamt of seeing whilst I can, rather than seeing the inside of a concrete mixer on my self-build project. I will see people who will become friends, people I would never have ever seen.

To travel simply, to work with compassion, to cement new friendships and to plant a legacy that will last years after my bones are gone! Walking the Camino has helped clarify a route from first steps in Vigo to vertigo on New Zealand's highest summit, sometime in the next two years. Perhaps I will meet you there?

Brad - Real Name Mike Harding

Why the Camino?

Several years ago, a friend gave me a DVD entitled 'The Way' starring Martin Sheen and directed by his son Emilio Estevez. He told me this film was 'right up my street'.

I thanked my friend and popped the DVD onto my bookcase, intending to watch it later. There it sat, I'm embarrassed to say, for a number of years. One day when I'd run out of other things to watch, I picked it up, dusted it off and watched it. I was hooked.

I'd always wanted an adventure with a capital A. I had dreamed of the Appalachian Trail. That was until 2017, when a car ran me down. I spent six months learning to walk again and another three years of treatment, and I was left with permanent nerve and ligament damage to one side of my body. My dreams of adventure were shattered.

However, 'The Way' showed me there was this thing called the Camino. I still wanted that adventure. The idea had never left me and kept buzzing inside my head like an annoying fly. I thought, why not? The Camino is very well established and isn't in the wilderness, so getting off the trail wouldn't be an issue if things went wrong.

So with just five weeks to prepare, I went for it.

My Experience

My experience of the Camino was pure joy. Even before it began, I was in Biarritz, unable to speak much French. However, using Google Translate, I went into a traditional French bakery and ordered lunch and some takeaway sandwiches. I've never enjoyed ordering sandwiches so much. The young lady serving me loved the app, and we had a giggle using it.

I think my experience of the Camino was such a joy because I had no expectations. With only five weeks of planning, how could I have? So for me, everything was magical. I met some truly wonderful people who changed the way I look at the world. I saw some magnificent landscapes and architecture first-hand and tasted terrific food.

My Advice

My advice would be to keep an open mind and do some research but not too much – you really don't need to know everything. Otherwise, surprise and wonder are diminished.

My advice for preparation is to do some shake-down walks fully loaded and get used to what you'll be carrying. Learn as much Spanish as you can well before your trip, and pack light – you will not need as much as you think, so leave the cast iron frying pan at home.

Camino Magic

In closing, for me, this journey wasn't just physical. As someone who registers on the Autism spectrum, social interaction is like an alien language. However, the need for nature and adventure drew me to the Camino. There were those along the way that I imagine tired of my incessant talking, something I am prone to do to fill a void of silence. For me, silence in a social situation equates to disapproval, as it makes me feel I've missed something and committed a social faux pas.

However, by the end of the Camino, I'd stopped caring what others thought of me. I just decided to be me. And here's the real magic... I found that some people liked the real me.

Lloyd Hart

My Experience

Walking a Camino for me was a lot simpler than most. I never really delved into anything spiritual about this pilgrimage, but I admired/envied people that did and enjoyed their faith. I am very happy to share the thoughts that transpire while walking.

Meeting fellow hikers, such as the author Julia, has always been an important personal factor. Enjoying the communal evening meal and the camaraderie of the day's struggles, whatever these may have been, has always filled me with a pleasure you can only find while hiking with other people. For whatever reason someone chooses to hike, it is never that much of an issue for me. It takes a certain type of person to enjoy a long-distance hike, and I enjoy sharing the experience with them.

My first Camino was the Portuguese way, from Porto to Santiago, about eight years ago, and it was a great chance to share a walk with my brothers. We have all enjoyed various hikes over the years, and now with young children and work life, getting away is a struggle. Planning a walk and enjoying a week or so with close family is the plus in all this.

When I have walked, it has never been for longer than 12 days. Long enough, some might say! So, planning the full Camino Francés took quite some time and came with many struggles. Three years ago, my hips were in absolute agony while walking long distances. I repeatedly tried to walk through the pain, but it wasn't meant to be. I had no option but to agree to a double hip replacement, each hip replaced a week apart.

My main fear while arranging an 800km hike was whether the hips would last the arduous journey I was planning. Luckily, they were fine, but issues with my feet quickly became apparent. The blisters were as bad as I have ever had or witnessed, and that, mentally more than physically, was the challenge I faced. With painkillers, great support and a strong, stubborn attitude, I managed to walk through the pain.

What I take away from a Camino, as with similar challenges, are the highs and lows that occur many times every day. At one end of the spectrum, you have the mental block of 'Why am I doing this? Why am I putting myself through this?' At the other end of the spectrum, there's utter euphoria in what you're achieving. For me, typically, that comes from a view I know anyone that wasn't keen to hike would never have the chance to enjoy from a car.

I arrive at a destination each day with such joy, reflecting on what I've seen, talked and laughed about with fellow hikers and appreciating the hospitality I often find. Walking a long hike, for whatever reason, has an abundance of ups and downs. If you can take the lows and look forward to the highs, you're meant to be on that hike.

My Advice

Where most pilgrims falter is the equipment. What also became apparent early in the hike is that you don't need as much as you will inevitably bring with you. You don't need that extra pair of shorts or warm jumper. You really can make do with the minimal amount of equipment without ignoring medical supplies for the blisters and feet issues, of course. The rule of thumb is to carry the least weight possible.

That said, having a jar of Coleman's mustard to hand to turn a very average ham sandwich into something substantially more enticing is absolutely worth the extra weight. Anything that can improve a meal is worth it, in my view. Spicing up a very boring soup can make all the difference in a meal. Fellow pilgrims might well frown at this concept, but I bet they ask for some as Julia did...

Anyone that escapes a Camino with no feet issues is a lucky person. We had one such lady I was lucky enough to meet, who was very kind in helping me when I was so down and out. Hazel became quickly known as Nurse Hazel and helped me tremendously, both physically and mentally. Kindness like that is in abundance on the Camino.

Marie-Josée Lapierre

Why the Camino?

The Camino project came unexpectedly. In the spring of 2022, I left a difficult work environment, feeling physically exhausted and mentally depleted. I was 46 and nowhere near retirement, even if it was a recurring thought during my previous gig.

What next? I decided to postpone my job search until the end of summer to pause, reflect on my next steps and recharge. I started exploring what options I had to fully enjoy this time off. My husband, friends and family were all working, and my teenage kids had summer plans. I would have to make a plan on my own. Travel? Go back to school? New career? Everything was open, and I needed time to focus on who I was and where I wanted to go next.

Thinking about not negotiating my agenda, going as I please and not taking care of anyone but myself suddenly became the best self-care plan I could think of. I had travelled to exotic places like India, Tanzania and Peru with friends or my husband, but organising and haggling my way for a change of scenery appeared too daunting a task. I needed a mental break, not a logistic nightmare.

I had had experiences with spiritual retreats and meditation through yoga. I had sought and found meaning and purpose through spiritual practice and was, and still am, on a faith journey to get closer to God. The thought of being alone appealed to me, and I needed time to be in my head, to think about my next steps, and to open up to something bigger than myself. I also thought nature would be a great remedy and possibly a healthy way of grounding myself. I have always enjoyed walking in the mountains – it makes me feel connected.

I read blogs on the Camino and saw that people of all ages were doing it. The physical challenge seemed reasonable – there were people much older and in much worse shape than I was doing it. I decided that my Camino would start in Astorga, 260 km from Santiago de Compostela and that I would walk for two weeks. I did not want to impose on myself a set number of kilometres to walk in a day. If I could not get to Santiago to catch my flight, I would take the bus – this was a break, not a work project.

My Experience

I did not reserve any hostels to allow myself to be in the moment and respect my limits. I arrived in Astorga after a flight, a train and a bus, with a super light backpack and good trail walking shoes. It was around 7.30 p.m., and the Episcopal Palace of

Astorga was still open. I felt like popping in. Why not? The freedom, the curiosity and the excitement took over me.

People were super friendly in the hostel the first night, but getting to sleep was a challenge. I was restless and nervous – I had not slept alone in 20 years! I was uneasy until I heard some snoring that made me feel like I was in a wolf lair, safe and surrounded by other fellow humans. The next morning, I was ready to conquer the trail, even if I didn't know where the day would take me. I enjoyed waking up before sunrise. It felt like a privilege to have the trail to myself, with the moon or my headlamp to guide me until the sun rose. The rhythm of the walk and the silence of the trail was soothing, like a meditation.

Since I only had two weeks, I had identified a list of questions to noodle over during my walks to guide my thoughts and make my walks intentional. I was hoping the trail would bring about answers. And it did. Every day after walking a couple of hours alone, I met pilgrims. After quick introductions, the anonymity of the trail allowed for immediate deep and sincere conversations on the reasons for embarking on the Camino – no time wasted for small talk. It made each encounter sincere, raw and authentic, like therapy from those who share a walk. I was privy to learning from fellow pilgrims through deep conversations about how to find meaning in life, get over the hurt of failure, find light after loss, and survive traumas from toxic relationships.

It helped me rebuild my foundation, remove the labels I had given myself and take the experiences that had left marks as what they were – events that occurred to me but that do not define me as a person. I reconnected with who I was and enjoyed it! The proverbial '¿Todo bien?' that pilgrims ask when meeting fellow walkers reminded me that I was safe if something happened to me. It made me feel part of a community, giving me hope in humanity.

I also found friendship on the trail, care from my friends when my feet got bad, laughing until I was crying, and crying with a listening ear. I was looking for meaning, and I found that on the Camino: true connection is the most fundamental need and purpose in my life.

My Advice

Make your bag as light as possible. You don't need a lot, and there are stores if you are missing anything. Don't put pressure on achieving a distance. The point is the journey, not the destination or the Compostela (certificate of completion). This is your first Camino, and you probably will have an opportunity to come back and see more. Care for your feet (bring supplies like lamb's wool, alcohol and needles). These are all very light, and this is the one thing that I really struggled with. I was blessed that Hazel and Julia were there as my feet saviours!

Reflect on why you are taking on this journey. It is an extraordinary opportunity for self-reflection and connection if you let it be that. Remember that it is **your** Camino. Set your boundaries and tailor it to your personal objectives, not those of a guidebook or other walkers.

Léya Lepage

Last winter, my aunt walked the Camino de Santiago by herself, and when she returned to Canada, she said to me, 'I want you to do it with me.' I understood that as a hypothetical 'one day' sort of comment. Yet, less than a year later, I was on a plane, leaving North America for the first time, mentally preparing myself for my 290km walk from Porto, Portugal to Santiago de Compostela, Spain.

Unlike many, my motivation to embark on this journey was strictly external. I feel no religious or spiritual connection to the Camino. I wanted to do this purely out of curiosity and wanderlust – I was presented with an opportunity for adventure, and I dove in head first, almost clueless. I had no preconceived opinions about the Camino, so I had no expectations at all.

The past few years of my life have been full of such uncertainty. Many people surely relate. I feel like the coronavirus pandemic robbed me of such important years – I missed out on the full potential of my last year of high school and my first year of university. Needless to say, I was feeling stir-crazy. Somehow, however, I don't think I consciously thought about it enough to know it. The Camino allowed me to do that.

Many people who've walked the Camino de Santiago or done other long hiking trips will say that it's the perfect opportunity to be mindful, meditate and look inwards. That's exactly what I did. During the 12 days it took to walk to Santiago, I developed a pretty good routine. My aunt and I would wake up and immediately get ready for the day. During the walk, we sometimes talked or sang, but for a large portion of the day, we walked in silence. At the end of the day, after we'd settled in our hostel, showered and eaten, I would journal. I wrote about the events of the day, but also how I was feeling and what I had been thinking about. My little green notebook is full of memories and secrets now.

I was also able to share my thoughts with the people I met on the way. The idea of a Camino family is very real. It's so encouraging to spend time with people who are focusing on the same goal as you; wake up, walk, sleep and repeat! As I look back on the people I spent time with on my Camino, it seems unfathomable that I only spent a few days getting to know them. It's easy to be vulnerable with others when you're all wearing the same stinky clothes day after day!

It's true – the Camino is not all fun and games. It is not easy to be rained on all day, to have blisters all over your feet, and to carry all your things in your backpack all day. That is also why it felt so rewarding to me. Being from the prairies of Canada means I'm used to hot, humid summers and harsh cold winters. I walked the Camino during the rainy season, and unfortunately, no Canadian weather prepared me for the torrents that came down on us. Having wet feet all the time was not fun and left me with some very intense blisters... But I pushed forward every day. Adventures like this certainly help one's body and mind establish new benchmarks for stress and tolerance.

Although the lows were low, the highs were magical. Upon her return to Canada after her first Camino, my aunt had said that she wished for a Camino for everyone. While I know the Camino itself may not be everyone's cup of tea, the transformative experience of embarking on an adventure and facing a true challenge is something that everyone should have the opportunity to experience in their lifetime. May we all have the chance to discover ourselves and the world around us, even amidst the challenges of our journeys.

Maida Maderazo

I met Julia and Mike while walking my fourth Camino, the Camino Portugues (Central Route), including the Variente Spiritual. This variant added three days to my Camino. It starts in Pontevedra and merges back into the Camino Portugues in Padrón. I started my Camino in Barcelos in Portugal and walked for ten days.

Why the Camino?

I look forward to walking the Camino for adventure and for spiritual reasons. A few months before I start my Camino, I get excited preparing for my trip. I look forward to doing my long walks/hikes at my local park as part of my training, especially when I start hiking with my backpack on the trail because I know my Camino trip is coming up. As I have come to realize, the different Camino routes are all new to me, yet when I am on the Camino, I feel at home. My mind is calm and clear, and I am more mindful. I come home feeling recharged.

My Experience

One highlight was the Variente Spiritual, although I did not see a single pilgrim. The route is just magical, and my stay at the Monasterio de Santa María de Armenteira was humbling. I even received a blessing from the priest and the nuns.

Other highlights of this Camino are visiting a new place by doing a new Camino route, meeting new people, sharing a meal with them, and not going to Finisterre and Muxía alone.

A lowlight was getting stomach flu while on the Camino. I had no appetite, and it made me restless.

My Advice

Make sure you have good footwear because it can make or break your Camino. Try walking with your shoes and backpack with the most miles that you plan to do while on the Camino. I had to go through three pairs of shoes/boots and hiked with my backpack for 15 miles before deciding that my feet were happy with trail running shoes with Injinji toe socks. I was also mindful of when I was getting hot spots on my feet while training, so I would use foot powder and blister tape on my next hike as a preventative measure. Using a pair of hiking poles lessens the impact on my knees on the downhill trek and helps me propel on the uphill hikes. I never had blisters on my Camino. I also increased my attendance at Bikram (hot yoga) classes to maintain flexibility, balance, and endurance. 'Yoga is lotion for your motion.'

I keep a mindset of 'expect nothing, appreciate everything'. Plan, but be flexible. The Camino provides! Even though things might not go how you wanted them to, in the end, things will work out for the best. It's true what they say 'the Camino will give you what you need, not what you want.'

A Final Word

If the Camino is on your bucket list, move it to your 'book it' list. If the Camino is calling you, go!

An Invitation

Congratulations on reaching the end of your Camino journey!

If you have enjoyed this book, then you will also enjoy **Live Your Bucket List**, which details the four-stage process outlined in Section 3 and includes stories from walking England's 630-mile South West Coast Path. You might also find **Walking The Camino: Supplementary Workbook** useful when planning your own Camino. It covers all the questions posed in this book, with space to note your answers. You can pick these up wherever you usually buy books from. You can download a shorter pdf, **Planning Your Pilgrimage,** and a sheet of **book club questions** from my website free of charge: www.juliags.com/camino.

You can listen to the introduction and first three chapters of **Live Your Bucket List**, also free of charge, at www.juliags.com/liveyourbucketlist.

I always appreciate receiving feedback so I can make the next version of this and future books better. I love hearing what you have to say — please leave me an honest review or email me.

And if you are looking for an inspiring and entertaining speaker for a meeting, event or broadcast, please give me a shout.

julia@juliags.com

www.juliags.com

@juliagsauthor

@juliagsauthorspeaker

@juliagsauthorspeaker

Acknowledgements

T
hanks to Mike for your unwavering support of my adventures and for walking the Camino with me.

Thanks to my Camino family for your company, insights and support while walking, and for taking the time to write about your experiences: Hazel, Mike P, Catarina, Mike H, Lloyd, Joe, MJ, Maida, Mimi and Léya. Thanks to Sara for contributing your thoughts about how to choose a Camino. Thanks to all my Camino friends who are too numerous to mention individually – you all helped to make the experience special.

Thanks to Teresa, for holding us in your heart; I think of you often. Thanks to Pepe and the staff at Albergue San Antonio de Padua in Villar de Mazarife, for your healing care. Thanks to Tim, for opening up the church at Molinaseca and welcoming pilgrims. Thanks to Arthur, for your beautiful paintings and prayer. Thanks to the team at the Pilgrim House in Santiago for the practical and spiritual support you offer pilgrims. Thanks to

Michele for sharing with me your thoughts about the energy of love.

Thanks to the staff at Debbie's Villas for making sure we had a roof over our heads for the final few nights on the Camino Francés.

Thanks to my launch team, readers and online supporters. Your ongoing support means a lot. A specific mention should go to Michael Heppell, Team17 and the Write That Book team who have helped me in my quest to be brilliant.

Thanks to Fern for continuing to inspire me and keep me on track.

Thanks to Jon Doolan for editing and challenging me to improve my writing, to Alejandro Martin for cover design and interior formatting and to Mark Lowe for recording and producing the audiobook.

Books by
Julia Goodfellow-Smith

Live Your Bucket List series
- Live Your Bucket List: Simple Steps to Ignite Your Dreams, Face Your Fears and Lead an Extraordinary Life, Starting Today
- Cycling King Alfred's Way: A Piece of Cake?
- Walking the Camino: A Journey for the Heart and Soul
- Walking the Camino: Supplementary Workbook

Walking guidebooks

- 15 Short Walks on the Malvern Hills, Cicerone Press
- Top10 Coastal Pub Walks: South Wales, Northern Eye Books

www.juliags.com/writing

About the Author

Julia Goodfellow-Smith is an ordinary person who is doing something extraordinary — living her bucket list. In recent years, she has discovered a love of hiking, which is why she leapt at the chance of walking the Camino.

Julia has held a variety of management and consultancy roles in a range of sectors including conservation volunteering, banking and construction. She is currently focusing her attention on adventure, writing and presenting.

Julia lives in Wales with her husband Mike, and loves their daily walks along the beach. She is a member of Rotary International, a Fellow of the Royal Society of Arts and a Senator of Junior Chamber International (JCI).

Julia is an AI-assisted author. For the production of this book, she has used AI for research (search engines), grammar-checking (Grammarly) and to help with producing the description of the book for marketing.

.

Printed in Great Britain
by Amazon